FAMOUS JERKS
OF THE BIBLE

Margaret Brouillette

FAMOUS JERKS OF THE BIBLE

BROADMAN
& HOLMAN
PUBLISHERS

nashville, tennessee

0-8054-2432-6

Published by Broadman & Holman Publishers, Nashville, Tennessee

Dewey Decimal Classification: 220.9
Subject Heading: BIBLE—BIOGRAPHY / CHRISTIAN LIVING—TEENS
Library of Congress Card Catalog Number: 2001035112

Unless otherwise stated all Scripture citation is from the NIV, the Holy
Bible, New International Version, copyright © 1973, 1978, 1984 by
International Bible Society.

Library of Congress Cataloging-in-Publication Data
Brouillette, Margaret, 1958–
Famous jerks of the Bible / Margaret Brouillette.
    p.   cm.
ISBN 0-8054-2432-6 (pbk.)
    1. Bible—Biography—Juvenile literature. 2. Bible stories, English.
[1. Bible stories.] I. Title.
BS551.3 .B76   2001
220.9'2—dc21

2001035112
CIP

1 2 3 4 5 6 7 8 9 10 05 04 03 02 01

ACKNOWLEDGMENTS

This has been an exciting project for me, and I couldn't have done it alone. Of course this book, the Bible, and life itself would have no meaning without a loving Father who pushes and prods jerks likes me in the direction of wisdom. And he has placed some great people in my life to help.

Thanks to Pierre, Laura, Sara, and Andre—my husband and children—for being a part of my life, for making me laugh and cry and love, for making me . . . me.

Thank you Rebecca Heron and Ginette Cotnoir—talented writers, extraordinary friends—for bookstore café meetings and phone calls and E-mails. Thanks for letting me ramble on about writing a book when nobody else knew what I was talking about and believing it really could happen when I wasn't sure anymore.

Thank you, Joel Buchanan, for having the rare combination of biblical knowledge, discernment, and youth to test the Bible study so ably.

And to Vicki Crumpton and the wonderful people at Broadman & Holman Publishers who said they might look at my manuscript if I was willing to risk the postage on a long shot, thank you. It was worth the stamp.

And now, thanks to you, the reader, for undertaking an adventure with me into the Word of God.

DEDICATION

To my heroes,
Doris and Hugh Buchanan—Mom and Dad

CONTENTS

INTRODUCTION
WHO'S A JERK?

There are a lot of stupid people around. Some people think they're hot stuff, that they're better than everybody else, that they don't need God. Some people have the truth about God's love and power in their face for years, but they never seem to get it. Some people live with their brains on hold and their passions on high. Solomon in the Book of Proverbs called these people fools.

I call them *jerks*.

Jerks are everywhere—in your neighborhood, on your team, in your club, at your school, at your church. And unfortunately, sometimes in your mirror.

The Bible is loaded with jerks. Some people are called by God and used by God, but their attitude stinks. Others are godless and unbelieving from beginning to end. Some have learned about God for years but can't see past themselves to put the truth into practice. A few smarten up before it's too late. Most follow the path of sin and end up in the sewer.

The jerks of the Bible all have major character flaws that contribute to their ruin. Getting to know the people and their sins is a good way for us to learn to avoid the same mistakes.

Every chapter of this book gives one jerk the opportunity to tell his or her story. Then you have the chance to figure out what

1

this person did wrong, what the Bible has to say about it, and how you can head in a different direction.

The story is an easy read. The Bible study may take a little more time. Don't rush. It's not important to get through a chapter in one sitting. It's probably not even a good idea. When you come across a truth or a challenge that you need to work on, stop. Take time to think it over. Put the book down and pray for God to change that area of your life. Make an effort to put the lesson into practice. Then pick up the book where you left off and keep going. You might want to try a chapter a week. That way you've got the time to let the lessons sink in, to reread the story in the Bible itself, and to learn a few verses by heart.

If you want to get more out of this study, do it with some friends. Work on the same chapter individually and then get together once a week to talk over the things you learned and pray for the steps that each of you wants to take in his or her life.

Each of the jerks in this book had a chance to change. Most of them chose not to. As I wrote about their lives, I recognized my own weaknesses in them. God is using this study to change me. I am still working on putting many of these lessons into practice.

Now it's your turn.

CHAPTER 1
THE HERO IN THE MIRROR

Nebuchadnezzar's Story
(DANIEL 1–4)

I am a king. I used to be a vain, proud, and conceited—not to mention hardheaded—king. But God just kept working on me. I still have problems with my inflated ego, but at least I finally figured out who's boss.

Call me Neb. The rest is a little hard to pronounce and even harder to spell. (Don't ever do that to one of your kids.) I'm from Babylon. A few years ago my army attacked the city of Jerusalem and overtook it. I asked my chief officer to find the smartest, healthiest, classiest young Jewish men and bring them back to Babylon. He did.

After three years of the best training possible, four of these guys really stood out. Their names were Daniel, Shadrach, Meshach, and Abednego. We thought they were a bit quirky at first because they refused our finest meat and wine. I can live with a vegetarian as long as he's a smart vegetarian. And these guys were *very* smart. I grilled them personally, and I was impressed. They were ten times better than all the magicians and enchanters in the whole kingdom. And the one called Daniel could interpret dreams.

To realize how stupid I was, you have to remember that Daniel understood dreams, and his three friends were practically brilliant. I started having dreams—weird, troublesome dreams. And I couldn't sleep. Ruling a kingdom is hard enough when you've had your beauty rest, but after a few all-nighters, the stress gets to you. So being an intelligent king who just recently hired a group of geniuses to work for me, guess what I did. I asked Daniel and his friends for help, right? Wrong. I called the old magicians to come and help me.

I told them about my nocturnal misadventures and asked for help. They said, "Sure. Tell us your dream, and we will tell you its meaning." I said, "No. You tell me my dream." They said, "You tell us the dream." I said, "You tell me my dream." They said (under their breath), "Are you crazy?"

Feeling slightly stressed, I warned that if they didn't reveal my dream to me, I would cut them in pieces and destroy their houses, for starters. They complained that I was asking too much. Being king, I was unaccustomed to dealing with criticism. I decided to have the whole lot of them killed—all of my wise men and even the four Hebrew brains. Not only was I eliminating the incompetent ones, I was going to kill off my only hope of ever getting an answer to my dream problem.

Fortunately Daniel came to me and said, "Excuse me, your majesty. If you wouldn't mind putting down your spear and sending away your henchman for a few minutes, I have a favor to ask. This dream mystery the whole kingdom is buzzing about—could you give us a chance to think about it before chopping off our heads?"

It was a long shot, but I was desperate. My own sorcerers had said that only the gods could interpret dreams, so they were no help. Maybe my vegetarian friend had connections.

Talk about connections! Daniel told me my dream in such detail that I felt like I was watching a rerun. He said I saw a huge statue, made of gold, silver, bronze, iron, and clay, in that order, from top to bottom. A huge rock smashed the statue, which blew away in the wind. And the rock grew.

That was it! That was my dream.

The meaning of it all was prophetic—foretelling the future of various kingdoms. What I liked the most was the part about me being the golden head, endowed with dominion, power, and might.

Daniel got a promotion for that one, with some luxury items thrown in. And then I put his three buddies in charge of Babylon's business.

Not only that, but I, King Nebuchadnezzar, actually said something smart. I said, "Surely your God is the God of gods and Lord of kings." Unfortunately, I didn't have enough brains to let him be Lord of *this* king.

With barely a verse in between to catch my breath, I decided to make a ninety-foot statue of yours truly for all to see and admire . . . and (this is really embarrassing) *worship*. So after the hoopla and the fanfare, every living soul was commanded to bow down to a piece of shiny metal and adore it.

Daniel's three friends in Babylon said no, plain and simple. I was seething. I tried to shake them to their senses by reminding them that no god was worth frying for.

But those gutsy kids stood their ground. They looked me square in the eye and said that their God was able to deliver them. And as if that wasn't enough, they said it didn't really matter, because they would keep on loving him anyway, even if he let them roast. That's when I exploded. They'd be torches.

Well, maybe you know this story. I was wrong again. And God was glorious again. Make that miraculous, awesome, astounding. The furnace was heated seven times hotter than usual. The men were dressed in formal attire for the occasion. They were tied by my strongest men and thrown into the flames. The heat was so great that it killed the guards who threw them in. But Shadrach, Meshach, and Abednego went in and out of the furnace without even frazzling a whisker.

Not only that, but they had time to entertain while they were in there. When we looked at the blaze, there were four men walking around as if they were strolling in the park.

I almost learned my lesson. I praised the God of Shadrach, Meshach, and Abednego. I even gave them credit for showing the good sense to side with God and stand up to me. That was more than humbling.

But, believe it or not, I wasn't humble for long. Or any smarter, for that matter.

I had another weird and wonderful dream. What would be the obvious thing to do? Yes, you're right, but I didn't. I called all my magicians and sorcerers first. When none of them could tell me the meaning of my visions, I finally turned to my last resort: the dream expert with the heavenly hotline.

The result was rather shocking. Believe it or not though, God was giving me one more chance. He sent a dream to warn me that if I didn't get over this love affair with myself quickly, he would take away my position, my power, and even my dignity.

I would live outside like an animal for seven years. I would act like a cow and have cow friends. I would eat grass and get wet. I would grow my hair out like feathers and my nails like claws. Disgusting. All I had to do was to admit that God was bigger than I was and the whole thing was just a dream. Seemed simple enough.

Unless you have an ego like mine.

One day, as I was looking over the city of Babylon, I was feeling quite cheeky. I uttered words like "might," "glory," "power," and "majesty" in a sentence with "I" and "myself." I'm sure you realize what happened next.

His royal highness became a local lowness in nothing flat. I found myself under a tree chewing weeds and growing my fingernails. I got wet. I got cold. I got what I deserved.

It took a lot of mistakes on my part and a load of miracles on God's part, along with seven years in a pasture, for me to learn one simple lesson. Now I think I've got it straight:

Now I, Nebechadnezzar, praise and exalt and glorify the King of heaven, because everything he does is right and all his ways are just. And those who walk in pride he is able to humble.

TAKE ANOTHER LOOK

Nebuchadnezzar was a slow learner—a conceited fool. Sound like anybody you know? I've got to admit that there are times when I look in the mirror, and I could swear that it's Nebuchadnezzar looking back at me. What is wrong with him, and what is wrong with me?

Nebuchadnezzar Had a Problem with Self-esteem

"Love yourself." "Respect yourself." "Build your self-esteem."

Today's experts tell us: if you just feel good about yourself, you will be a good person—a friendly, active achiever. But it didn't work for Nebuchadnezzar. He felt good about himself, but his "self-esteem" was the cause of his misery and sin.

The Bible has a lot to say about your worth. You are not the product of millions of years' worth of genetic mistakes. God created you. That's not all. He created you to be like him and, even more astounding, to be loved by him! Read 2 Samuel 22:20 and Psalm 149:4. What do these verses say about God's feelings for his children?

_____

_____

So go ahead—feel good about yourself!

OK, OK—enough already. If you pat yourself on the back too long, you will need a reality check. Look at these verses describing the evil and corruption that inhabit your heart: Romans 3:23, Isaiah 1:5–6, and Jeremiah 17:9. Write a summary statement:

_____

_____

That's balance. Have you noticed that the Bible is a lot better at balance than the society around us? And did you notice that the four talented Israelite vegetarians (who suffered no inferiority complexes) were better at it than the old king?

Self-esteem is cousin to pride; and in the murky waters of psycho-speak, it's often hard to tell the difference. But for the sake of clarity here, let's put self-esteem on hold and take a closer look at pride, which is certainly only a short step away.

Pick a word or two out of each of these verses to show what God thinks of pride:

Proverbs 8:13 _____

Proverbs 11:2 _____

Proverbs 16:5 _____

Isaiah 2:12 _____

James 4:6 _____

Pretty clear, isn't it?

Paul spells out the balance in black and white when he writes, *"For by the grace given me I say to every one of you: Do not think of yourself more highly than you ought, but rather think of yourself with sober judgment, in accordance with the measure of faith God has given you"* (Rom. 12:3).

Do you have a balanced opinion of yourself? What are your best qualities? (Find positive character traits rather than natural talents—e.g., playing the violin is a talent, being generous is a character trait.)

_____

_____

What are your weaknesses? (e.g., I get mad easily; I am lazy.)

_____

_____

You should get the idea here that you're not all good, but you're not all bad either. You're not perfect, but you should be improving. God wants that list of positive character traits to get longer and the list of negatives to get shorter. Paul says it this way in Philippians 1:6: *"He who began a good work in you will carry it on to completion until the day of Christ Jesus."*

When you start to feel pretty good about the changes in your life and the progress you are making, don't let it go to your head. Remember the words of Jesus: *"Apart from me, you can do nothing"* (John 15:5).

Nebuchadnezzar Had a Problem with Humility

If pride's a bad thing, then we should probably be working on humility. The problem is, for all of us incredible creatures of God, loved and cherished and going to heaven, humility is hard to pin down.

For starters, it would be easy to say that humility is the opposite of pride. So if pride is an inflated evaluation of my own worth, humility would mean believing I am worthless. Wrong.

So try a different angle. Humility comes with important fringe benefits. Maybe understanding the results of humility will help us understand what humility is. What do the following verses say?

Proverbs 11:2 _____

Proverbs 29:23 _____

Psalm 18:27 _____

Psalm 25:9 _____

1 Peter 5:5 _____

Now we know the perks, but we still don't have a definition. Humility, like love, exists only when it's active. So the next step is to answer the question: *What does humility do?*

The only perfect example we have of humility, along with every other virtue, is Jesus Christ himself. He alone was truly humble in ambition, attitude, and action.

Read Philippians 2:3–7 two or three times, slowly, and then try to answer the questions below.

Ambition = What are the two expressions that describe the opposite of humility in the first sentence (v. 3)? _____

_____

Does that sound anything like "getting ahead," "climbing the ladder," "looking out for number one," or "being all that you can be"? Check your own ambition meter. Are you using the gifts that God has given you to promote yourself, or to serve him and others? With 10 being serving God totally and 1 being thinking only of yourself, rate yourself between 1 and 10 here.

_____

Attitude = If I am humble, what attitude will I have toward other people (v. 3)? _____

> *There is a great man who makes every man feel small. But the real great man is the man who makes every man feel great.*
>
> —G. K. Chesterton

Does that mean that somebody else's opinion might be right, even if it is contrary to mine? Does that mean that the guy who is less athletic or the girl who is less popular could be just as correct as I am? You got it. Is that the way you feel already, or are you out there strutting your stuff and fighting for your rights? Give yourself another score of 1 to 10 for your attitude toward others. ____

Actions = If I am humble, how will I act toward other people (vv. 4, 7)?

_____

_____

What is a servant? Somebody whose sole purpose is to meet the needs of another person, right? Somebody who sacrifices his own comfort and reputation for that of another. And in Jesus' case, somebody who sacrificed the very superior role and honor he deserved to rescue very unworthy human beings. How do you compare?

- Do you look out for other people's interests?
- Do you make a conscious effort to meet others' needs?
- Do you go out of your way to make other people look good?
- How much would you be willing to give up to help somebody else?

Give yourself a score of 1 to 10 for showing humility through your actions. ____

How did you do on these three questions? What could you do this week to improve that score and imitate Jesus' example of humility? Do you need to change your ambitions, your attitudes, and your actions? How?

_____

_____

An accomplished pianist once gave me a picture of humility that I have never forgotten. Although she was sought after for piano solos, she preferred to accompany vocal soloists as they presented great songs of worship and praise in church. She said her challenge was to play so well that the singer would sound better and the song would be more meaningful, and that she would go unnoticed.

Ask yourself: *Do I do the things I do to be heard and seen, or so that others will be heard and seen . . . and appreciated?*

Nebuchadnezzar Had a Problem with Worship

Nebuchadnezzar had the wrong hero—himself. He had the nerve (and the power and the money) to build a statue of himself and command other people to worship. I don't imagine I'll ever do that, exactly. But, oh how many times I have wanted approval, praise, and admiration. I want to make sure everybody knows when I've done something important or good. And I want to get the credit for all the ideas and projects that work, and still avoid the blame for the ones that don't.

My problem and Neb's problem center on something we call "glory." What other words come to mind when you think of glory?

Did you come up with words like *praise, elevation, honor, splendor, acclaim,* and *superiority?*

Look at these verses, and see how many other words you can find that go along with *glory:* Exodus 15:11, 1 Chronicles 29:11–12, 1 Timothy 1:17, and Revelation 5:12–13.

_____

_____

_____

Did you notice that the common thread in these verses is that they are all songs and prayers of worship? Giving glory means to worship, and that kind of adoration belongs to God alone. He says himself that he will not share glory, and he has a good reason. *"I am the LORD; that is my name! I will not give my glory to another or my praise to idols"* (Isa. 42:8).

Nebuchadnezzar wanted that glory. He wanted to be worshiped. He loved himself to the point that he accepted and even expected the recognition and praise of others.

But Nebuchadnezzar eventually understood. It took seven years of living like a wild animal. The day he was restored was the day he took off his "hero" badge once and for all and gave it to God.

In answer to the question, "What is the chief end of man?" the Westminster catechism replies, *"Man's chief end is to glorify God, and to enjoy him forever."* Paul writes in 1 Corinthians 10:31, *"So whether you eat or drink or whatever you do, do it all for the glory of God."*

How can you eat and drink for the glory of God? What does it mean to worship in the routine of daily life?

_____

_____

What about you? Does the way you live give glory to God? What can you do differently to worship God by pointing others away from yourself and to the only one who is worthy of praise and adoration?

_____

_____

CHAPTER TWO
DYING TO CONTROL

Haman's Story

(ESTHER)

If you like a story with a happy ending, skip this one. This is a tragedy. I should know—it's my tragedy. I'm going to the gallows—me, Mr. Nice Guy. And I still don't know what went wrong.

This is how it all started. King Xerxes, the rich and powerful (and conceited) ruler of our land, decided to show off again. Only this time he outdid himself. He spent six months displaying his accumulation of glitter to visitors from all over the world. To top it off, he threw a seven-day party. This was an all-you-can-eat, all-you-can-drink bash; and believe me, when it was time to leave, nobody was sober enough to get back up on his camel and drive home.

By day seven the boys were ready for a visit from the girls; and Xerxes, who had a beautiful wife, decided to put her on parade. So there we were, waiting to get a look, and she had the nerve to let us down. Vashti—that was her name—refused to come and dance for us. Who ever heard of a woman saying no to a man?

The king sent her away with a severe warning to all the wives in the kingdom not to follow her example. Then the king chose a new wife from all the beautiful girls in town, and they were supposed to live happily ever after, and the rest of us too.

Life would have been so easy after that if it were not for Mordecai. He obviously doesn't recognize greatness when he sees it, because he won't bow down to me. And he's a snoop and a tattletale.

Like the time two of the king's officials, pretty good guys if you ask me, came up with an idea to get rid of the old royalty. Don't get me wrong. I always say that "your majesty" stuff to his face, but between you and me, Xerxes is starting to lose it. Somebody with my charm and ability would be better suited to the job.

So Mordecai, who always sits at the palace gates, overheard the plan and told Queen Esther, who warned the king. My two buddies were hanged like criminals, and Mordecai's name was recorded as if he were some kind of hero.

Now the good side of that little episode was that I got a promotion. I was named number one nobleman, just as I deserved. The king commanded all the royal officials who hang around the gate to bow down to me. It's a nice way to start work on Monday morning.

But guess who wouldn't comply? Mordecai, the scoundrel. That's when I found out he was a Jew. They have a thing about not wanting to bow down to anybody but their God. How narrow-minded can you get?

The solution was obvious. Getting rid of Mordecai would

not be enough. All the Jews had to go. So being the brilliant man that I am, I devised an awesome plan.

I played to the king's weak spot—his pride. I let him know that a certain group of his subjects were not cooperating. They refused to obey the king's laws. Well, one of them, anyway. When I got the king heated up to boiling point, I offered to put some of my own money into the treasury to pay for the elimination of the troublemakers. He loved it, and I came out shining.

The command was sent ahead of time so everybody would be ready for this convenient genocide. Who should care anyway? Jews aren't important. I figured that the only people who really counted were in the king's court, so nobody would notice if we just threw out the riffraff.

I should have been right.

I sat down with old Xerxes to have a glass and relax, but we had to close the windows. Those Jews are noisy when they're upset. I did have the pleasure of seeing Mordecai wearing rags and ashes. He wandered and wailed, and I enjoyed.

Things got better. Three days later the Queen invited the king and me to a special dinner. Then she invited us back the next day! It was just the three of us, and I was on top of the world. At least I would have been, without Mordecai. He still wouldn't bow down to me—the nerve!

When I got home, I invited all the high society types over to let them know how privileged they were to be my friends. I explained in appropriate detail all the honors the king had given me. But I had to end my recital on one sour note—you know who. My little woman and our company had a great idea. Build a gallows. Hang him the next day. Go for dinner in peace. Good riddance. Great plan.

I went to see Xerxes the next day about this hanging

idea, and before I got a chance to speak, he asked me a loaded question.

"What should the king do for someone he wants to honor?" he said smiling.

I was sure this was my big chance, so I laid it on really thick. It had to be me, and I knew how I wanted to be treated.

"Give him a royal robe and a royal horse with a royal crest. Parade him through the city shouting, 'This is the man the king wants to honor.'"

I could already feel the attention and admiration.

The king's answer came as a total, disgusting shock. "Do all this for Mordecai, the Jew."

Pardon me?

It seems his majesty got up for a midnight snack, started to look through the old royal records, and discovered that Mordecai had never been rewarded for saving his life from the two schemers at the gate. Now I had to put a royal robe on this guy and lead him around on a royal horse shouting that the king honored him.

It was the longest afternoon of my life.

I ran home feeling sick. When I told my friends about it, one of them warned me that the whole thing smelled a little rotten.

The king's messengers interrupted my pity party by whisking me off to my dinner appointment.

I had no appetite.

While we were drinking a little wine, the king, who was in a very good mood, promised to give the queen whatever she wanted. When she spoke, my dreams were shattered. My worst nightmares were surpassed.

Esther told King Xerxes there was a plot to kill her and all her people. It turns out the queen is a Jew! In fact, she's Mordecai's cousin!

I felt like I was in somebody else's movie, acting out somebody else's screenplay. This was not the way I wrote the story. Somebody else was in control, and I didn't like it at all.

You can probably guess what happened next.

Xerxes said, "Who's the villain?"

Esther pointed to me and said, "The adversary and enemy is this vile Haman." Gulp. I turned green. The king turned red. He left his wine and stomped out into the palace garden. I could tell his mind was made up.

I was desperate. I went over to the queen and got down on my knees and begged for mercy. The king came back in the room and thought I was making a move on his wife. When he said, "Will he even molest the queen while she is with me in the house?" I knew it was the last straw.

Then some bright boy said that there was a seventy-five-foot gallows in my backyard. Wouldn't that be a funny place to hang me?

Ha. Ha.

It's over now. They have covered my head. I'm on my way to be hanged on the gallows I built for Mordecai. I was right, but everything went so wrong. Why do such awful things happen to nice people like me? It's not fair; it's just not fair.

TAKE ANOTHER LOOK

Haman was right. He was playing a role from a script that somebody else wrote. And for a guy that was a control freak, it was a hard pill to swallow. Especially when he ended up digging his own grave, or at least building his own gallows.

It's too bad Haman didn't take the time to listen to God's people and inquire into the source of their faith. He would have learned that he wasn't really in charge of his own life. None of us are.

Haman Wanted Control

Haman had no notion of God. He expected to run his life, control his circumstances, and organize the people around him. This obsession shows up in Esther 3:5–6: *"When Haman saw that Mordecai would not kneel down or pay him honor, he was enraged. Yet having learned who Mordecai's people were, he scorned the idea of killing only Mordecai. Instead Haman looked for a way to destroy all Mordecai's people, the Jews, throughout the whole kingdom of Xerxes."*

First of all, Haman expected to be honored. Second, he was insulted to the point of wanting to kill Mordecai simply because he did not bow down. And then, as if that wasn't enough, he decided to wipe out the entire Jewish race. Haman was a jerk because he completely missed the obvious. He didn't see God at work until it was too late.

The Book of Esther is great reading because of the story line, the intrigue, the characters, and the reversal at the end. But it is also the only book in the Bible that never mentions the name of God, while being completely drenched with his person and his plans.

God orders and controls the universe and our lives. If you're not convinced (and even if you are) see what these verses say about his plans:

Job 42:2 _____

Psalm 33:8–11 _____

Psalm 115:2–3 _____

Proverbs 19:21 _____

Haman was not in charge of his own life. Neither are you. That means that no matter how hard you try to change your family, your teachers, or your friends or how hard you look for the perfect computer, job, roommate, boyfriend or girlfriend, chemistry partner, or college, somebody else has the last word.

Not only does God run everything, but he has no obligation to explain himself to you or to me. A lot of us, like Job and his friends, could carry on for thirty-seven chapters trying to understand and explain our circumstances, typically excusing ourselves, judging others, and misrepresenting God. I love the last five chapters of Job. After listening to a lengthy discussion about his character and actions, God breaks into the conversation. The remarkable thing is, he never answers the question "why?" But he does ask a few questions of his own.

"Job, were you there when I splashed the heavens with stars?"

"Do you know where light lives?"

"Can you feed lion cubs and ravens and donkeys?"

"Do you understand how animals give birth?"

"Do you make the birds fly?"

"Do you know what death is like?"

The amazing vision of the vast creative power of Almighty God is the Lord's way of saying, "My name is God. Your name is Job. Any more questions?"

How would you do on an exam like that? Job stutters and falters and repents. He has caught a glimpse of majesty and learned a lesson in humility. So

> *A fool can no more see his own folly than he can see his ears.*
>
> —William Thackery

Haman, if you think you're the boss, think again. You have no idea who our God is.

That is what Paul means when he writes that awesome praise chorus:

> Oh, the depth of the riches of the wisdom and knowledge of God!
>
> How unsearchable his judgments, and his paths beyond tracing out!
>
> "Who has known the mind of the Lord? Or who has been his counselor?"
>
> "Who has ever given to God, that God should repay him?"
>
> For from him and through him and to him are all things.
>
> To him be the glory forever! Amen. (Rom. 11:33–36)

Write your own song or prayer, praising God for his extraordinary power to control the universe and our lives.

_____

_____

_____

Haman Thought He Would Win in the End

The Psalms and Proverbs are full of promises that the righteous will be blessed, vindicated, and sustained while the wicked will be cursed. God's ultimate justice is a great theme throughout Scripture. And a straight reading of the Book of Revelation should convince anybody that terrible disaster and glorious relief are on their way. It is essential to be on the right side because, despite temporary appearances to the contrary, the good guys will win in the end.

Take a look at Proverbs 10, the whole chapter, and fill in this chart with the contrasts you find between the wicked and the righteous.

Verse	Wicked	Righteous
1	_____	_____
3	_____	_____
4	_____	_____
6	_____	_____
7	_____	_____
9	_____	_____
16	_____	_____
21	_____	_____
23	_____	_____
24	_____	_____
25	_____	_____
27	_____	_____
28	_____	_____
29	_____	_____
30	_____	_____

In a world where some non-Christians are decent people and so many Christians are making compromises with the world, it may be hard to tell the difference. But God knows. And some day he will separate the sheep from the goats, and the wheat from the weeds, as Jesus promised.

Haman thought he was going to win. But he didn't. Are you really sure which side you're on? Think about it.

Haman Did Not Do God's Will

If Haman knew these two important facts—God rules, and the good guys win—he would have been more interested in cooperating with God's will.

There has been a lot of discussion about finding the will of God, and some question as to whether it has ever been lost! Perhaps we should talk less about finding it and more about doing it, as the Bible does.

A good place to start is in 1 Thessalonians 4:3, the first part of the verse. Copy it here.

_____

_____

Two elements in the Christian's life will guide him toward holy living or "sanctification"—which, after all, is what the will of God is all about. Can you find them in these two verses: Psalm 40:8 and Psalm 143:10?

_____

In these two: John 17:17 and 2 Thessalonians 2:13?

_____

It should come as no surprise that in Ephesians 5:17–19, Paul says to understand God's will, be filled with the _____

_____

and speak and sing together the praises of God. When he wrote about the same subject to the Colossians, he said to be filled with the _____

(3:16) as we teach one another and sing praises.

God repeats in the New Testament the point he makes in the Old Testament, just to make sure we understand. Doing God's will depends on being filled with his Word and his Spirit.

What do you think it means to be filled with God's Word? What are the best ways to do this? Make a list and then check the ones that you are already doing.

- _____
  _____
- _____
  _____
- _____
  _____
- _____
  _____
- _____
  _____

What are you going to do about the others?

_____

_____

This is a little trickier. What does it mean to be filled with the Spirit? Maybe Ephesians 5:17–18 and Galatians 5:16 will help you out here.

_____

_____

Controlling and energizing is the Spirit's job. Submitting and obeying is mine. Sin comes from "the flesh." Works of righteousness come from the Spirit. Lining up my desires and actions with those of God will result in supernatural power, along with some very visible character traits. Paul refers to the fruit of the Spirit as love, joy, peace, patience, kindness, goodness, faithfulness, gentleness, and self-control (Gal. 5:22). Does it sound like he's talking about you?

The apostle gives us another perspective on being directed by the Spirit of God when he says to Timothy: *"For God did not give us a spirit of timidity, but a spirit of power, of love and of self-discipline"* (2 Tim. 1:7).

Is God's power at work in your life? Are you conscious of supernatural strength?

Is God's love so real in you that you sacrifice yourself to serve others?

Are you self-disciplined? Do you control your emotions and passions and deliberately do what is right?

Which of these areas do you need to work on? Ask God to help you.

Haman Made Bad Plans

The good news is that God has a blueprint for your life. He knows exactly what college you will go to, if and whom you will marry, and what you will accomplish for his kingdom. The bad news is, you will never see a copy of that plan. (Even if you did, like Job and Paul you would say, "You're too big for me and I don't understand any of this!")

If you are reading and memorizing Scripture and following the Spirit's guiding as he applies those truths to your life, you still don't know if you should buy a car or a motorcycle, major in science or English, or go to camp or your uncle's in the summer. Right?

You have to make a choice. Please note that you are allowed to make mistakes here without sinning. Bad choices that are not the result of bad character are OK. God is ultimately more interested in your heart than your Harley or hatchback anyway.

What are some things you should keep in mind as you make decisions?

Proverbs 14:22 _____

Proverbs 20:18 _____

Matthew 6:33 _____

Luke 14:28 _____

1 Corinthians 10:31 _____

James 4:13–17 _____

Do you have a decision to make or something to plan? Pass it through the test of the passages you have just read. Pray about it. What seems to be the best choice? Why?

_____

_____

_____

CHAPTER THREE

PLAYING A LOSING GAME

Judas's Story
(MATTHEW 6:14–56, 27:1–10)

I felt betrayed. I devoted three years of my life to this guy. I believed in him. I thought he could do it. He had what it took to save our people. But he turned soft. Started talking about suffering, dying. We've had enough suffering. What we need now is for the Messiah to come and save us from these wretched Romans.

Jesus was an unlikely candidate at first. He was the carpenter's kid. They were a nice family—commoners, but well respected. Everybody imagined that Jesus, being the eldest son, would take over his dad's business.

That's why it was a bit of a surprise when he went out to see that radical cousin of his and asked to be baptized. The story is that the people standing there saw a dove come down and heard a voice from heaven. They claim God said that Jesus was his own son. Pretty impressive credentials if it was true, but everybody knows that Joseph is his father.

Crowds of people started to follow him, and I went along. He fascinated me. He was different. He obviously had more in him than making furniture. He spoke of power and kingdoms and God's children. That would be us—the sons of Israel. He became immensely popular. I saw him heal lepers, calm storms, and drive out demons. Jesus had power. Even if his comrades looked second-class, I became more and more convinced he had the charisma and the call from God to be our deliverer. With help from a military mind like my own, he was sure to win. He seemed to think so too.

The day he came to me and told me to follow him, I was ready. He spent the night in prayer and then officially chose twelve of us. I was surprised at a few of the guys he picked, but I figured it wouldn't really be a problem as long as they didn't get in the way. Of course, crowds of people continued to follow him; but we were, let's say, the elite.

He even sent us out on missionary trips. He gave us power to heal diseases and cast out demons. Our message was simple: "The kingdom of heaven is near." What a rush! If Messiah could make the blind see, what would it be like when he decided to take the throne of Israel and throw out the Romans! He himself said that things would turn nasty at some point. "Do not suppose that I have come to bring peace to the earth. I did not come to bring peace, but a sword"—those were his very words. Believe me, after seeing the miracles Jesus performed, I planned to be on the right end of that sword when it started doing its job.

I did think Jesus' idea of hotel accommodations was a little misguided when he started dragging us around the countryside and sleeping in the open air. As for food, well, let's just say he ate when it was available but didn't get overly concerned when it wasn't. They say he spent forty days without food or water after his baptism. Starvation is not my calling. Of course, Susanna, Joanna, and their friends tried to keep the meals coming, but that was pretty irregular.

Good thing I handled the money. That way I knew I could always take care of myself in a pinch. Jesus didn't seem to pay attention to the bookkeeping. Some of his followers made donations, and I carried it all around in a bag. I figured it was my job to make sure that bag never got too heavy. We certainly didn't want the Master and his fishy friends to be weighed down by material things. Anyway, a lot of that money was intended for the poor, and I'm sure you'll agree that anybody who slept on a rock fell into that category. It wasn't stealing; it was just redistributing the wealth.

Well, time passed. Jesus talked less and less about kingdoms and more and more about crosses. He was constantly at odds with the religious leaders who should have been the first to put their seal of approval on the Messiah. Some of his miracles were for outsiders—a Samaritan woman, a centurion's servant, a Syrophoenician woman's daughter. Those seemed like a waste of his time to me.

The more I got to know him, the more I realized he didn't have a bone to pick with Rome, either. He even said we should pay our taxes, to "give to Caesar what belonged to Caesar."

One day it dawned on me that this was a dead-end street. I had left everything and spent three years with this guru. Jesus was a fake. He had no intention of saving the people. He was no liberator. He was a loser. And I would not waste any more time with a loser.

I made my decision. I was at the end of my rope, and something inside me just snapped. It was the stupidest thing I ever did.

I knew that the chief priests hated Jesus. I also knew that the crowds loved him. The religious leaders wanted to get rid of him, but they were too scared to capture him in front of the foolish masses. The people still believed the Messiah story. I was starting to see things the priests' way.

If Jesus couldn't do anything for his nation, I decided I would. I went to the chief priests secretly, to tell them where they could find Jesus alone with his disciples after the Passover meal. I felt betrayed. I hated him. I wanted to get rid of him. But I just couldn't bring myself to do it. So I sold him. I asked for thirty pieces of silver—the price of a slave—and I promised to take them to him when he would be far from the crowd.

And then I went for dinner.

That Passover was a strange meal. We were all there—the regulars, I mean. John, who was teacher's pet, was leaning up against Jesus. Peter, who had the annoying tendency of talking when he didn't know what to say, was doing just that. I was on the other side of Jesus, planning my exit, imagining my meeting with the priests. Now that I had decided to get out of this sect, nothing could stop me. I was obsessed.

I knew that Jesus could read people's minds, but I wasn't expecting what happened next. After we sat down for supper, he announced that he would be handed over to the authorities and that one of his disciples would betray him. How did he know? Well, even if I hadn't fooled him, the other guys were confused. They all started asking, one after the other, if it could be them. So I joined in by saying, "Surely not I, Rabbi?" like the others. Except this time Jesus answered, "Yes."

Eleven men in that room must have been more interested in eating than playing detective because either nobody heard, or nobody caught on. When Jesus urged me to go quickly, no one seemed surprised. Maybe they thought he sent me to buy more food.

I knew exactly what I had to do. I went to the chief priests. I told them Jesus would be heading to the Garden of Gethsemane, where he liked to get away with his special friends. I pocketed their money and we left together.

We rounded up a crowd of Jewish leaders, Roman soldiers, and curious onlookers, and we paraded into the garden. The crowd was huge, and I was in front. Finally I would do something important. Jesus stood there like he was expecting us. The disciples looked more ready for a coffee than for a fight.

The prearranged signal was a kiss. Even in the darkness of the garden, it was easy to pick out Jesus. I approached him, said, "Greetings, Rabbi," and kissed him. He called me "friend."

Dear old feisty Peter seemed to wake up all of a sudden. He got mad and tried to chop off a guy's head. He only got his ear. Jesus told Peter to put his sword away. Then he put back the servant's ear as if nothing had ever happened. I was right. Jesus didn't have it in him to overthrow the Romans. He was too soft. Too undecided. Too weak.

So they took him away.

They tried him in the night. They reached a guilty verdict, of course. The verdict was reached before they ever seized him. And now he will die.

He healed the soldier's ear. He raised Lazarus from the dead. He blessed the children.

He called me "friend."

I spent three years following him, and I've never seen so much power, so much compassion.

Maybe Jesus isn't what I had hoped, what I had dreamed.

Maybe he isn't what I wanted him to be. But he is all I have. Jesus is innocent.

I betrayed an innocent man. And now he will die.

Thirty pieces of silver. Thirty stinking, rotten pieces of silver. "Cursed is the one who takes a bribe to slay an innocent person." That's what the law says. An innocent man is going to die because I sold him for thirty pieces of silver. I am cursed.

Where will I go? What will I do? What is money to me now? What is life to me now?

It's useless. It's hopeless. I'm finished.

TAKE ANOTHER LOOK

Judas Iscariot is a baffling character. He walked and talked with Jesus of Nazareth for three years and yet was able to turn his back on him. He was selfish and hypocritical and treacherous. So what was he doing with Jesus?

Judas Followed Jesus for the Wrong Reasons

In the Jewish mind Messiah was and still is a political liberator. The Old Testament predicts that the son of David will set up a kingdom that will be just, glorious, eternal, divine, and rule over all other kingdoms. When the Jews were under the heavy hand of Rome, only a miracle worker could get them out. Enter Jesus. He was a son of David. He spoke with authority. He worked wonders. And he said that the kingdom was at hand.

He also said that the twelve disciples would sit on twelve thrones. Judas wanted his piece of the cake.

But Judas misunderstood. Jesus clearly said to Pilate during his mock trial: "My kingdom is not of this world." We can't be too hard on Judas here because he wasn't the only one who didn't get it. None of them did. James and John even had their mother come and ask for special favors for her two sons in the kingdom. More than once the Gospels record Jesus asking his slow-learning disciples, "Are you still so dull? Do you still not understand?" And the answer comes back: "But they did not understand." Once when Jesus predicted his betrayal and death, Peter actually had the nerve to contradict Jesus to his face. All

> *He that serves God for money will serve the devil for more of the same.*
>
> —Anonymous

the disciples were confused on this point. Eleven of them still trusted Jesus.

Judas had another obvious weakness. What was his price for handing Jesus over to the chief priests (Matt. 26:14–15)?

_____

Read the account of the woman anointing Jesus with expensive perfume in John 12:5–6. What does this say about Judas?

_____

Judas followed Jesus for the wrong reasons—one philosophical and one practical. He wanted to be a part of a great political movement. He also wanted to fill his pockets.

Judas Overlooked an Amazing Privilege

The apostle John was also speaking for the other disciples when he said, *"The Word became flesh and lived for a while among us. We have seen his glory, the glory of the one and only Son, who came from the Father, full of grace and truth"* (John 1:14).

What are some of the awesome things that Judas saw and heard in person?

_____

_____

_____

Did you think of some of these?

* Judas witnessed miracles—healing, casting out demons, walking on water, calming the storm, feeding the five thousand, raising Lazarus.
* Jesus constantly outsmarted the Pharisees.
* The events of Jesus' life constituted a series of fulfilled prophecies.
* Judas heard radical teaching on self-sacrifice, materialism, prayer.
* Judas lived day and night with a perfect person.

In Matthew 13:11, 16–17, Jesus reminds the disciples of the special window they were getting on spiritual truth. What did Jesus offer to Judas and to the other disciples?

_____

Not only were the disciples witnesses to God's truth and power, but they also were participants. What does Mark 6:12–13 say about the mission of the disciples, including Judas?

_____

I have never seen anybody walk on water, but I have had opportunities to get to know God—some that even Judas didn't have. What about you? What are some of the people, experiences,

events and things in your life that have given you a chance to
know God?

- _____

- _____

- _____

- _____

- _____

Judas did not appreciate the privilege that was his. In fact, he
rejected the truth he saw and heard about God. Are you like Judas?

Judas Played the Game

It is amazing to me, and scary, that up until the last minute
none of the other disciples even suspected that Judas was an
impostor. When Jesus said clearly at the last supper, "One of you
will betray me," the disciples each asked in turn, "Is it me?"

These guys had been living together, doing miracles
together, following Jesus together for three years. And Judas
played the part so well that nobody knew what he had in his
heart.

How is it possible to fool so many people for so long?

Maybe some of the teachings of Jesus will help us understand. Read the parable of the weeds and the wheat in Matthew
13:24–30 and the explanation in verses 37–43. Are there fake
Christians among us? _____

When will they be "weeded out"? _____

Judas heard Jesus serving the Pharisees up for lunch in
Matthew 23 as he continually blasted them for being hypocrites.
Read verse 28, and picture how it applies to Judas.

How was he like the Pharisees on the outside? _____

_____

How was he like the Pharisees on the inside? _____

_____

What is the warning in Mark 4:22 that applies to Judas, all other pretenders, and maybe even you? _____

_____

It is clearly a terrible thing to fool other people into thinking you are something that you are not. It is worse when you fool yourself. In Matthew 7:21–23, what are some of the reasons given by those who want to enter the kingdom? _____

_____

Looks good, doesn't it? Certainly Judas would qualify. But at the judgment Jesus will say, "I never knew you." Who is it then that will enter the kingdom of heaven?

_____

Judas Rejected the Savior

Let's face it, none of the disciples were glowing examples of Christian piety. They were selfish, petty, slow learners, who all eventually denied Christ in one way or another. But eleven of them were restored. Eleven of them believed. Eleven of them turned back to Christ.

Judas regretted his awful act but turned away from the one who could forgive. What do these verses say about the end of Judas' story, physical and spiritual?

John 6:70 _____

John 17:12 _____

Acts 1:18 _____

You, like Judas, have had many opportunities to get to know Jesus Christ. In fact, you know that Jesus rose from the dead; Judas didn't stick around long enough to find that out. You have the complete Word of God in your hands—Old and New Testaments, the life of Christ, the letters of the apostles to the early church, and the Revelation of things to come.

Judas didn't have any excuse for rejecting the truth. Neither do you.

Maybe you are just playing the game. Nobody knows what's really in your heart. Or so you think. But Jesus does. And he still wants to call you "friend." You can get away with pretending to be a Christian for a while. But you're really just a weed in the wheat. Someday everybody will know.

Judas thought he would be important and powerful. He wanted to be rich. He wasn't ready to make the sacrifice to follow Jesus all the way. He never really understood how to live, even after hearing it from the mouth of Jesus Christ himself.

"Whoever finds his life will lose it, and whoever loses his life for my sake will find it" (Matt. 10:39).

"What good is it for a man to gain the whole world, yet forfeit his soul?" (Mark 8:36).

Are you a follower of Jesus? Are you just on the fringe looking in, wondering if you're ready to give away your life? Or are you a pretender, fooling your family, your friends, and maybe yourself? Give up your petty ambitions. Hand your life over to a loving God who will wipe away all your guilt because the consequences have been paid by the sacrifice of his Son. Live and walk in obedience, free from yourself and devoted to serving others.

If you have never done it before, pray now to ask God's forgiveness and dedicate your life to being a disciple of Christ. Write the date here: _____

Now go tell somebody what you have decided. *"If you confess with your mouth 'Jesus is Lord,' and believe in your heart that God raised him from the dead, you will be saved"* (Rom. 10:9).

CHAPTER FOUR
DRIFTING TOWARD DISASTER

Lot's Story
(GENESIS 13–14,19)

I never imagined it would end this way. Yes, we had our ups and downs, but I thought we were finally getting settled. All I wanted was a good life for my family and me—a few friends and that comfortable feeling you get when things are running smoothly.

Of course, Abram and I didn't see eye to eye on that one. We were different in so many ways. I wonder where he is now. I wonder if he's even heard about the disaster—my friends, my city, my wife.

I really used to admire my uncle. I still do, I guess. It's just that he was always such a dreamer. Don't get me wrong. I believe in God and everything. I mean, if I didn't, I wouldn't have followed him in the first place.

When Uncle Abe, Aunt Sarai, and I left Haran, it was because God had told my uncle to go. "Pack your bags and

41

leave." The funny part was that we knew where we were coming from but didn't exactly know where we were going. It was hard to make travel arrangements.

"Hello, is this Haran Camel Caravans? Yes, I would like to make reservations for three in your next tour. Pardon me? Yes, as soon as possible, from Haran, for three adults. Do you have seniors' discounts? Good, we'll take two seniors and one regular, please. Where to? Not a clue. How long? Beats me!"

We set out in the direction of Canaan, and we arrived in . . . Canaan. We kept losing Uncle Abe because he'd go off to pray. He built altars here and there across the countryside and whispered things to Sarai about promises and descendants and land.

After a while I got pretty rich, and so did my uncle. We both had herds and flocks and servants, and it was getting hard to find a camping spot. Abram and I seemed to be able to talk things over, but our servants didn't share a family tree as we did. They were more interested in getting a good night's sleep than in negotiating. After a while, to the sound of bleating and lowing, diplomacy went down the drain. To keep peace among our animals and our servants, something had to be done. It was time to go our separate ways.

Uncle Abe, being rather generous but not much of a businessman, gave me first choice of the land. I looked east and saw lush land. The plain of the Jordan was like a garden. I looked west and saw desert. It was an easy choice. I went east.

I set up camp for my family, my servants, and my expanding mobile meat supply not too far from the town of Sodom. I had heard the place had a bad reputation, but I figured there was nothing wrong with taking advantage of the green grass in suburbia.

Before long we tired of fresh air and good water and bought our little house in the city of Sodom. The first crisis struck shortly after.

There was an age-old feud going on between two groups of kings, and I ended up in the middle of it without really understanding what was happening. The city was captured, and the people were dragged off by four kings with impossible-sounding names. Since we were now residents, we got captured with everybody else.

Uncle Abe came to the rescue. He rallied an impressive gang of soldiers, chased the hoodlums down, and captured us all back. He even recovered all the stolen possessions and brought the women and kids back home safely.

Life got back to normal after that round of excitement, and I didn't hear from my uncle for a while. I got quite a reputation for myself in Sodom and rose to a role of importance. I was seated among the elders, judges, and dignitaries at the city gate. It seemed to happen naturally, and it felt good.

I was at my place one day when a couple of strange-looking visitors came along. Strange and strangely familiar, like something out of my past. Now I want to make clear that I was offended by the behavior of the people around me, and when it got really bad, I sometimes had to turn my head. You just learn to put up with certain things. Besides, gray only seems really dirty when you hold it up against white.

When these strangers came to town, I saw white. They reminded me of Abram. They reminded me of God. They made me a little uncomfortable sitting at the city gate of a town full of homosexuals. How could I hide what was going on there? How could I come out looking clean? I'd have to try to sneak them into my house and sneak them back out.

When the two newcomers said they were planning to spend the night on "the Main," I thought I'd die. I had to make them change their minds; I could feel disaster coming. I laid on the bit about my wife's good cooking and our warm house and clean beds until finally, to my relief, they agreed to come with me. Things were running really smoothly until just about bedtime. Would you believe it—all the men from the whole city of Sodom, young and old, surrounded the house. And they weren't exactly there for a hymn sing. It was a nightmare.

"Where are your visitors?" they called. "Bring them out so we can have sex with them!"

I have never been so humiliated. How could I quiet down the mob? How could I keep my status in Sodom and still play the good guy to these squeaky clean visitors? How could I please everybody?

To understand what I did next, you have to try to put yourself in my place. I was in panic mode. I had backed myself into a corner. I had no choice. I had spent so many years just trying to be popular. And now there was a chance I would lose everything. So I played my last card: my daughters. Yep . . . I offered my two virgin daughters to the men on the porch, if they would just leave my visitors and me alone. That way, if I could keep them happy, I might still have my desk at the gate on Monday morning. And my overnighters wouldn't have to know a thing about it. They turned down my little proposal.

The men started saying that I was just an outsider and had no business telling them how to live. A little heckling I could have dealt with, but they were trying to break down the door to take the guys by force.

By this time it was obvious to everybody that I was in

trouble. The visitors could plainly see what kind of scum I had been associating with, but it was too late to save my reputation. I was trying to save my life. And theirs.

As it turned out, I couldn't even be the hero. They were. They pulled me back inside, locked the door, and struck every man and boy on the street with blindness.

I was breathing heavily. They were talking quickly. "We have been sent by God to destroy this city. Get your family together and run. And hurry."

I was in no position to argue.

I went out to the crowd and found my future sons-in-law. I told them to pack their bags, and they laughed at me. Poor kids.

At dawn, the two snow-white men, who I had figured out were angels, told us to *scram, vamoose, get out!* I paused, and they pushed. They grabbed my wife, my two daughters, and me and practically dragged us out of there.

"Now get going," they urged. "Don't stop. Don't look back. Run to the mountains. And do it now!"

And I said, "Ah . . . do we have to?" It just didn't feel right. Of course, I thanked them for saving our lives and all, but after a rather brief discussion, I weaseled my way into moving to a cute little town on the plain. It was far enough away to be safe and just close enough to feel comfortable. I was sure mountain life wasn't for me.

The angels disappeared. The sun came up. We heard banging and rumbling and crashing. And we smelled the awful stench of something burning. We hightailed it out of there as if we had been training for the hundred-meter sprint. At least, I thought we did.

It was hardest for my wife. Hard to leave her friends. Hard to say good-bye to comfort and security. Hard to follow some foreign messengers of a God she had never seen. One minute she was beside me, running. The next, she was turning her head. I tried to call out. I tried to say no. But it was too late. She had left her heart in Sodom, and when she turned around to mourn it, she froze there. She became a pillar of salt—instantly. What could I do? I kept running.

I don't really know what I did wrong. I just followed my feelings. I always have. And now it feels so . . . lonely.

TAKE ANOTHER LOOK

Lot looks like a greedy, power-hungry, immoral man—a first class jerk.

The problem is, the apostle Peter doesn't seem to have read the same story I did. When talking of God's just judgment, he writes, *"He rescued Lot, a righteous man, who was distressed by the filthy lives of lawless men (for that righteous man, living among them day after day, was tormented in his righteous soul by the lawless deeds he saw and heard)"* (2 Pet. 2:7–8).

What is wrong with this picture?

If Lot was such a righteous man, why did he make so many compromises? If he hated the lifestyle of Sodom, why was he living there? If he believed in God, why didn't it show?

Assuming that Peter is talking about the same Lot I read about in Genesis, we have to accept that the Holy Spirit says that Lot was righteous. That means he was a believer and his intentions were good.

Lot's problem, then, wasn't willful disobedience but poor judgment—a series of bad choices. This was a man who followed his heart all the way to his own ruin and the complete upheaval of his family.

Lot based his choices on feelings rather than convictions.

Lot's Senses Dictated His Choices

Look at Genesis 13:10–11. "Lot _____

_____

and _____

that the whole plain of the Jordan was well watered. . . . So Lot

_____

for himself the whole plain . . . and set out toward the east."

This was a big decision. What did Lot base it on? On what he saw. And what he saw was "greener grass." A well-watered plain meant an easy life for shepherds. The fact that he was heading in the direction of Sodom and Gomorrah was irrelevant. He took what looked good.

You have a problem with this, and I have a problem with this, just as Lot did. It's obvious that taking the biggest piece of cake, wanting the prettiest Christmas present, and choosing the coolest toy comes naturally to all of us. Just watch any three-year-old (or thirteen- or thirty-year-old).

But grabbing whatever teases our senses can lead to big trouble, especially when the stakes are higher than chocolate cake.

What about clothes, cars, computers? What about friends? What about sex?

Can you think of a choice you have made recently, purely for pleasure?

Do you want to go through life choosing the biggest, the best, the most pleasurable—whatever the cost?

Take Moses. He was given a ridiculous choice: to be a prince or a slave. And he chose . . . slave. Read Hebrews 11:24–26. This is good! Moses chose to _____

rather than _____

Why? (v. 26) _____

_____

Senses and feelings are so demanding because they are present, urgent, now. Lot was influenced by the pull of immediate gratification. Abram and Moses were willing to believe God. They let go of present pleasure, knowing that something better was waiting in the long run.

Can you say with Paul, *"So we fix our eyes not on what is seen, but on what is unseen. For what is seen is temporary, but what is unseen is eternal"* (2 Cor. 4:18)?

Lot Was Influenced by the Woman in His Life

We don't know much about Lot's wife, but what we do know is significant. She looked back. You can take the girl out of Sodom, but you can't take Sodom out of the girl. If Lot's righteous heart was troubled by the sin of the city, his wife seemed to feel like she belonged.

Why did Lot move there if he was offended? Remember this guy is a follower, easily influenced. And who can influence a man better than a woman? Look at Adam and Eve. Eve was tempted by Satan. Adam was tempted by _____

Right . . . Eve. Samson lost his strength at the hands of _____

_____

That's it—Delilah.

See the pattern?

One of the obvious ways to avoid this pitfall is to decide way ahead of time to marry a dedicated Christian. That means that the guy or girl who charms your heart has to pass the test. If not, back off buddy.

Some of these questions might help:

Does the person who interests me romantically:

- Help or hinder my walk with Christ?
- Possess the character that I want my children to imitate?
- Have qualities I love that will still be there in twenty, thirty, fifty years?

Read Proverbs 4:23 and copy it here.

_____

_____

Now copy it on a card and put it in your wallet, in your locker, in your room (or all of the above).

Lot Did What Felt Good

"Follow your heart," they say. I don't know about you, but when I look inside, I see jealousy and discontentment, selfish ambition, and pride.

What does Jeremiah 17:9 say about the heart?

_____

What does Jesus say in Matthew 15:19?

_____

Following your heart is obviously not a good plan.

What body part is named in 1 Peter 1:13 and Romans 12:2?

_____

Why is the mind so important? The Christian is a Christian because of what he *believes*, not what he feels. Take a minute to recite John 3:16 if you need proof of that.

Renewing your mind is like tuning your brain to be in key with the mind of God. How can you do that? Look up and read all the following verses, and find the common thread.

Colossians 3:16a _____

Matthew 4:4 _____

John 17:17 _____

Ephesians 6:17 _____

Hebrews 4:12 _____

How can you renew your mind? _____

Do you know what you believe? Do you know your Bible? Do you read your Bible? If you want to fill your mind with God's thoughts, your first good choice should be to read it every day. Write here the time of day that you read, or plan to read, your Bible every day this week: _____

Lot Went Along for the Ride

Lot didn't know what he wanted. He followed. He drifted. He crashed.

Notice that drifters never drift up. Lot chose lush land. That seemed innocent enough. He moved close to Sodom. He moved into Sodom. He got involved in the politics of Sodom. His wife loved Sodom. He offered his own two daughters to the men of Sodom. Lot's life proves that moving with the flow usually gets us dumped in a swamp.

As Christians, we do not want to follow the flow. We are constantly exercising our will, making choices.

Do you know what kind of person you want to be? Is that the kind of person you are today? How would your friends describe you? _____

_____

How would your enemies describe you? _____

_____

Think about how you want to be remembered after you leave high school, college, or your summer job. What reputation would you like to have at church, at home, on your team? What do you want people to say about you after you die?

_____

_____

Now ask yourself this question: Does my choice of friends and activities contribute to making me the kind of person I want to be?

Lot Had No Convictions to Take Him Through a Crisis Situation

When you meander through life trying to please, it's easy to end up in a situation of conflict and not have any real values to pull you through. When your heart is pounding and your adrenaline is flowing, chances are your judgment is not very reliable. Always know what you believe ahead of time, and decide how you will act before the heat turns on.

Abram was like that. A funny thing happened when the king of Sodom wanted to give him a present after Abram saved him and his people from the attacking kings. Abram said, *"I have raised my hand to the LORD, God Most High, Creator of heaven and earth, and have taken an oath that I will accept nothing belonging to you, not even a thread or the thong of a sandal, so that you will never be able to say, 'I made Abram rich'"* (Gen. 14:22–23). He had decided long before that he would not

> *In matters of style, swim with the current; in matters of principle, stand like a rock.*
>
> —Thomas Jefferson

associate his reputation with Sodom. Too bad Lot hadn't done the same.

Abram had convictions. Lot didn't. Do you? Try to fill in some of these blanks for starters:

The next time my brother/sister gets on my nerves, I will

_____

When I am offered drugs, I will _____

When a non-Christian guy (girl) starts to show interest in me, I will _____

When I am tempted to look at pornography, I will _____

_____

Next time somebody laughs at my faith, I will _____

_____

If I know I can cheat on an important assignment without getting caught, I will _____

If It Feels Good . . . Think Twice

Feelings are important. Good feelings are great. Pleasure is a bonus. Just don't rely on your heart as a guide to holy living.

There is a better way:

- Make sure your mind has been regenerated by the Holy Spirit. That means becoming a Christian.
- Feed your mind with the Word of God.
- Think deliberately about pure things.
- Exercise your will by making good choices.
- Establish convictions. Plan ahead how to behave.

Then . . . *if it pleases God, do it!*

Learn Romans 12:2 by heart and repeat it to yourself the next time you have to make a choice.

CHAPTER FIVE
A PASSION FOR POWER

Pharaoh's Story
(EXODUS 7–14)

I have never lost a fight—before today. I am strong, mighty, powerful, and awesome. I am Pharaoh. When I sit on my throne and hold my scepter, I am filled with the spirit of the great god. In fact, I am god.

The day the white-haired guy and his brother showed up, I was congratulating myself on all the construction projects we had completed over the last few years. With those Hebrew slaves making bricks and building houses and temples, two new cities had grown out of the land. All to my credit, of course.

I have even surpassed my father in greatness and glory. When he saw that there were too many Hebrews, my father started up a family planning project—kill off all the little boys. But those people just kept on multiplying.

I, on the other hand, undertook a *city*-planning project. I know a good thing when I see it, and what I saw was free labor.

Let them have babies—boy babies especially—and let them work. From dawn to dusk. For me. That made my kingdom stronger.

That's why I was so unprepared when Moses and Aaron came to visit. They claimed they came by order of a greater God to command me to let the Hebrew slaves leave Egypt. Just lay down their trowels and walk away. No negotiations. Just "Bye-bye, boss!"

I was furious. I blasted out something like, "I don't know anybody by the name of 'the LORD,' and I certainly will not let your people go."

I gave new orders for the slaves to start gathering their own straw to make the bricks. By working them twice as hard, it would be easy to deal with the dreamers in the crowd.

Chalk up another victory.

Unbelievably, the same two senior citizens showed up at the palace again. They asked me to free the slaves—again. And I said no—again.

Then the smooth talker—Aaron—threw his cane down on the floor and it turned into a snake. I would not be intimidated. I called in a few of my magicians, and they had no trouble imitating Aaron's little trick. All of those magic wands turned into serpents before you could say "Abracadabra." (Of course, it did seem rather odd when that one little snake of the Hebrew fanatic ate all of the Egyptian snakes.)

The next morning I went down to the river to wash, and I got another shock. There they were, the belligerent brothers, waiting for me down at the Nile.

They sang the same old song, and the second verse was strangely familiar: "Let my people go."

I said, "In your dreams."

Aaron reached out his stick, touched the Nile just as I was washing my face, and the water turned to blood. Even the water in all our sinks and jugs turned warm and red.

So I made the Hebrews dig for water, along with making bricks and finding straw. I would show them who was boss. I didn't know this God they talked about, but I did know how to fight. And I got in a good blow.

A week later, to everyone's relief, the Nile cleared up. But the stench of the rotting fish along the banks could have raised a mummy from the dead. And my palace is right next door.

Well, I've got to hand it to the Hebrews: they're persistent. Moses and Aaron came back with the same order from the same God: "Let my people go."

I said no. And I paid for it.

I had never seen so many frogs in my life. They were in my food. They were in my pajamas. They were in my house and my fields. They were in my face. One or two I don't mind, but it was practically raining the little amphibians. So I struck a deal.

"Get rid of the frogs tomorrow, and you may leave," I promised.

The frogs dropped dead, and I changed my mind. After all, I am still Pharaoh.

I know the secrets of the pyramids. I know the art of Egyptian burial. I would like to know where Aaron got his stick. Because he took that thing, touched the ground, and all the dust turned into gnats. We could hardly inhale without getting a nostril-full of the little pests.

Just as I was picking some gnats out from between my teeth, I got the bad news that I had company. Moses, of course. He said his God would send swarms of flies all over Egypt, except the little neighborhood of Goshen where the Hebrews lived.

It happened exactly as he had said.

After that our animals got sick and died. And the Hebrew animals were all left standing.

We were being hit from every side. Again and again. I stood my ground. I am Pharaoh.

Next we got boils on our skin—runny sores all over our royal bodies. This was becoming intolerable. But I would win. I would find a way to conquer this phony power. Unfortunately, the next point also went to the Hebrews.

When the storm came and the hail fell, we had never seen anything like it. We lost half of our crops, which was scary since the animals had died and we had all become vegetarians.

After that the locusts came and wiped out what was left. It looked like a giant scythe had moved across our land. The ground was smooth. The fruit was eaten. The men were grumbling.

Then came the darkness. Total, terrifying darkness. We were unable to function for three whole days. And everybody wondered how long a nightmare could last.

When the light came back, I was a new man. Stronger and meaner. And determined to settle the score once and for all and prove my superiority.

I told the Hebrew harassers to get out of my sight and never come back. That is when the blow came that knocked us down.

The wailing woke me up. My magicians were crying, the people were crying, my wife was crying. My son was dead. In every household, every family in Egypt, the firstborn had died in the night. The heir to the throne, the future Pharaoh, the chosen one of the gods—gone.

We were down, and we were desperate. We practically chased the Hebrews out of Egypt. Our people begged and bribed them to go. And they did.

It was a moment of weakness I will always regret.

I shook myself out of my stupor, got up from the mat, and raised my fists again. Pharaoh never loses a fight. I am almighty. So I rallied my troops and sent them after the fleeing crowd. "Beat them up and drag them back" was their mission.

I went along to savor the sweet taste of victory. Tracking them was easy. We found them camped beside the Red Sea, telling stories beside a spectacular bonfire.

We headed straight for them. You couldn't miss that fire out in the middle of the wilderness. I can't exactly explain what happened next because fires don't normally jump from one spot to another. Not normally.

As we approached their beach party, the campfire that was on the other side of them disappeared and quickly reappeared on this side. That meant that a wall of fire was blocking our attack. I don't know if my face was red from the heat or from my rage.

As if we hadn't had enough, the winds came up like a tropical storm. Their mysterious deity somehow pulled off another of his magician's tricks. The Red Sea separated, as if a celestial comb came down and parted it like hair. The Hebrews marched right through the sea, on sand. The great army of Egypt followed in hot pursuit.

Here my story ends, and my confusion and humiliation begins. The waters rushed back together, and my entire army— soldiers, chariots, and horses—was lost. The fight was over. The God of the Hebrews had knocked us out and walked away.

I am Pharaoh, but my power is nothing compared to his.

TAKE ANOTHER LOOK

Pharaoh thought he was strong. He was right.

In fact, power was handed to him on a silver platter. He was trained to expect it. He ate and drank the servitude of others. He was the morning and the evening star. The sun rose and set on him and his decrees. He had the power to say that something was so, and history would be rewritten.

He also had inherited a taste for abusive force. His father had enslaved an entire race of peaceful inhabitants and ordered the slaughter of baby boys. He continued the tradition of domination. He increased the workload of the slaves. He refused to let the Israelites go, even though his own people were suffering from the plagues. He then sent an army to capture and slaughter the Israelites after their departure. His aggression only increased in intensity with his determination to maintain some sort of supremacy.

Strength can be a good thing. Leadership is admirable. Fighting is sometimes necessary. So why was Pharaoh such a jerk? What did he do wrong?

Pharaoh Fought the Wrong Enemy

If Pharaoh had taken the time to ask Moses a few questions, rather than dismissing his request as a charade, he would have saved himself a lot of trouble.

What was Pharaoh's own admission concerning God? (Exod. 5:2)

Imagine how different things could have been if he had gotten to know the God who came knocking at his door.

> *Power tends to corrupt and absolute power corrupts absolutely.*
>
> —First Baron Acton

Of course Pharaoh couldn't see into the future. He didn't know anything about Jesus' calming the storm or feeding the five thousand, or even the fall of Jericho. Neither did Moses, for that matter.

But if he had been listening while Moses' mother, Jochebed, rocked her baby and told stories of the Hebrew *Yahweh*, he would have learned that one unique all-powerful God spoke the word *Earth*, and the world came to be; he said *Stars*, and the heavens shimmered. When that same God declared what was right and wrong, no creature-king could contradict him.

God caused a great flood to destroy the earth, saving only a handful of social outcasts and their floating zoo. Who would dare lift a fist to that kind of power?

Once, a group of people wanted to make a name for themselves. They tried to build a tower that would reach to heaven. Then God changed a *yes* to a *oui* and a *no* to a *nein* and *friends* to *amigos* until the builders got so confused they abandoned their architecture and were scattered across the earth. *Adios. Au revoir.* Good-bye.

God adopted Abraham and promised to bless him and his descendents, even after they were displaced into a foreign land. Whose foreign land? Pharaoh's.

What did Joseph say to his brothers when he was on his deathbed? (Gen. 50:24) _____

Joseph was supernaturally protected and guided by God to bring his family into Egypt. If Pharaoh had known that God promised Joseph to lead them back out someday, he might have had Moses' passport ready the first time he came to visit.

Because Pharaoh didn't know God, he had no idea who he was challenging. He still held the illusion that he himself was invincible, "almighty." He was definitely the king of "de-Nile."

To get a better portrait of the God he was confronting, read Psalm 89:1–15. Now read it again, slowly. How many words for *strength* are used in verses 7–8 and 13? List them here: _____

_____

In Psalm 89:7, what tells you that God is way out of anybody else's league—whether human being or angel? _____

_____

Easy question: Would you want to be on the same side as the God described in Psalm 89? _____

Pharaoh Fought the Wrong Way

Pharaoh built strong buildings, and he hurt weak people. In his determination to establish the most awesome dynasty ever, he used and abused and massacred the most awesome creation ever. Not only was he violent, but he was temperamental—constantly changing his mind or his mood.

God's manner of wielding his power is very different. What two words does David use to describe him in Psalm 89:8? ____

_____

Mighty is strong. Faithful is trustworthy and reliable. No tantrums. No fits. He's strong, but he's steady. This is power you can count on.

What two qualities of God are named in the last part of verse 14 of the same chapter?

_____

How close do those words come to describing you? When you get worked up about something that you think is worth fighting for, can you honestly say you still act with love and faithfulness? God does.

Real love is a sign of true strength. Look up 1 Corinthians 13:4–7 and check out the description of God's kind of love. Now reread the verses in their adaptation below, and consider if this sounds like you.

I am patient; I am kind. I do not envy; I do not boast; I am not proud. I am not rude; I am not self-seeking; I am not easily angered. I keep no record of wrongs. I do not delight in evil, but I rejoice with the truth. I always protect, always trust, always hope, and always persevere.

Choose one of these statements that you know you need to work on. What can you do to show God's love in a situation that is difficult for you?

_____

_____

_____

Remember always to begin by praying for any person with whom you have a hard time. Thank God for his qualities, and ask God to bless him.

Pharaoh Used His Power for the Wrong Cause

Pharaoh had a cause: his own. Don't we all, sometimes?

Worst of all, we try to sign God up as a little foot soldier in our own army, ready to follow orders and fight for us under our wise direction and command! Listen to yourself pray (or complain) sometime, and you'll see what I mean.

What does Psalm 89:14 say that God's throne is built on?

_____

I have to wonder what I would build mine on, if I had the chance.

Take a look at your life and try to see what your foundations are—your major "causes."

These questions might help: What do you think about the most? What do you look for in other people when you compare yourself to them? What would you be willing to fight to defend? What do you spend the most time on?

_____

_____

_____

_____

_____

If your list looks anything like mine, it might include:

- My reputation
- Popularity
- Ambition for success in education, work
- Getting married
- Money
- Everything that makes me *feel* good

All of us invest some energy and worry into some of those things some of the time. And like Pharaoh we waste time building dynasties that will fall and forget all about the kingdom that will last.

What do you think are some of God's major concerns? What do righteousness and justice look like? Take a stab at it first, then look up the following verses: 2 Peter 3:9, Romans 12:1–2, Ephesians 5:27, John 17:22–23, Matthew 5:48, and James 1:27.

_____

_____

_____

_____

Did you come up with some of these?

- Spreading the good news
  of Jesus to the entire world
- My personal obedience
  . . . in everything
- The purity of the church
- Love
- Defending the poor and
  the weak
- Self-sacrifice

> *The love of liberty is the love of others; the love of power is the love of ourselves.*
>
> —William Hazlitt

If I find that I am getting a little too preoccupied with that first list and forgetting the second, I know I need to refocus. Have you been preoccupied with yourself? In what way? _____

_____

Do you need to spend a little more time and energy on righteousness and justice? Choose one of God's priorities that you could develop more in your own life.

_____

What are you going to do this week to work on this area?

_____

_____

_____

Supernatural Source

You've made up your mind. You want to get to know God. You want to live the right way. You want to work for the right cause. But where does the power come from?

Read Psalm 28:7 and Psalm 46:1. Rephrase the expression *"The Lord is my strength."* _____

_____

Read Ephesians 6:10. What does Paul mean by, *"Be strong in the Lord"*?

_____

Maybe you're a fighter. Maybe you're a leader. Or maybe you're the quiet, observer type. No matter who you are, remember that God is the one who has the power. And you can do some pretty great stuff together, if you stay on *his* side.

CHAPTER SIX

POWERED BY PASSION

Samson's Story
(JUDGES 13–16)

I was special from the beginning. And I knew it. When other parents were telling their kids stories about Noah's ark and the crossing of the Red Sea, I asked to hear the same tale over and over again. It was the story of the angel—the story of me.

My mom and dad were going gray, and they still didn't have any children. In Israel, where I come from, that's a curse. My mom had just started to accept that she would never have her own baby to burp or toddler to tweak. Then she had a visitor. An unusual man came by and told her she would have a son. She had to avoid drinking wine and eating pork chops because the boy would be a Nazirite. That means a kid on the fringe, chosen by God to be different. It also means no haircuts, ever.

My dad, who missed the visit, really wanted to hear this for himself. So he prayed and asked, pretending he wanted more instructions about raising a kid with long hair. And God answered.

When the big shiny man came back, he repeated the same things to my father. But that wasn't enough for Dad. He wanted a name and address—anything to identify the guy. That's when the stranger pulled the stunt that I still love to hear about. He told my dad to offer a sacrifice to God. When the goat and grains were on the barbecue, the visitor stepped closer to the rock where the fire was and then he just lifted into the air and disappeared in the flame. It was like he hitched a ride to heaven in a puff of smoke. Incredible.

Mom and Dad panicked because they finally realized they had seen the angel of the Lord, which usually meant instant death. One thing that reassured them was that God promised to give them a baby in nine months. He couldn't kill them and do that too.

I always felt strange growing up. Being a Nazirite meant I had to stay away from raisins and grape juice . . . and barbers. Besides, I was an Israelite, and the Philistines had captured the Israelites, so we weren't exactly upper-class citizens. The angel told my mom I would be used to help deliver my people. That's a pretty hefty mission, but I took it to heart. I was a colt trying to break out of its harness—always ready for action, anxious to show off my muscle. I felt a rush coming over me from time to time, and it gave me a feeling of invincibility.

My body grew, and so did my passions. (Know the feeling?) I took a little trip into the heart of Philistine territory and saw a gorgeous young foreigner. I decided I would have her. I came back and told my mom and dad to get her for me. They argued a bit about the advantage of marrying a nice Jewish girl, but they had always given in before, and they did again.

We left for Timnah together so I could introduce my parents to my newest conquest. On the way I got tangled up with a colossal cat, and he got the worst of it. I felt one of those power surges and tore that lion from limb to limb. My parents didn't see it, so I washed my hands and went for my date without breathing a word of it to anybody. The next time I took that highway, I saw the strangest thing—a swarm of bees and honey were there in the lion's carcass. So I did what any hungry young man in his prime would do: I helped myself.

When wedding time came, the party was almost as impressive as the groom was! The reception lasted for seven days—eating, drinking, and being very, very merry. I was supplied with thirty usher types to accompany me, but these weren't my best friends. They were Philistines, the enemies of my people. So I decided to have a little fun at their expense. I told them a riddle and asked for the answer during that week, wagering thirty linen garments and thirty sets of clothes, which was a little more than my honeymoon suitcase could hold.

Knowing what I have already told you, you'll probably get this riddle right away, but you can imagine why it was difficult for those guys at the feast. I said, "Out of the eater, something to eat; out of the strong, something sweet."

They had absolutely no idea what I was talking about, so they went to my beautiful bride and asked her to get the answer from me. She said, "Tell me the secret," and I said, "Why should I?" Then she clung to me and cried and pleaded. Do you know how long seven days can be? This was supposed to be a celebration, but my new wife just sobbed and begged day after day. Her eyes were compelling. Her perfume was dreamy. Her touch gave me goose bumps. She said, "You don't even love me."

That was it. I finally told her. She told her people. They answered the riddle. I lost the bet.

I was livid. How dare they humiliate me like that at my own wedding?

I rushed out of the banquet hall, killed thirty Philistines, and gave their clothes to my "companions." I passed my wife off to my best man and went back home to mother. No woman would betray me and get away with it.

In fact, I figured I could deliver Israel from the Philistines better without a woman in my life. I decided to put my hormones on hold and concentrate on the Lord's work. Simple as that. Sort of.

Before long those beautiful eyes and that dark flowing hair came back to haunt me. What a face. What a body. What a woman. I went to see her. And for some reason her father didn't want me to go to her room. The fact that she had married the best man might have had something to do with that. So he offered me her younger sister. I didn't want her; I wanted my woman, now. I was fuming.

And in a couple of hours, so were the Philistine crops. I caught three hundred foxes, tied their tails together, and stuck torches in the knots. The foxes went crazy and ran through the fields, vineyards, and orchards, sending the whole food supply up in smoke. The Philistines got so angry that they killed my ex and her father. I got revenge by slaughtering a gang of them. The stakes were going up, and I was determined to win.

The people of Judah, my own people, became so afraid of the revenge of the Philistines that they were ready to get rid of me. I gave them permission to tie me up and hand me over. I didn't want to upset the people I was trying to help, and besides, this was a little game that I would enjoy playing. Just at the right moment those ropes seemed to turn to threads. I gave a heave and was free—free and strong and hyped. I grabbed a donkey jawbone lying nearby and killed about a thousand Philistines.

A while later I had another romantic interlude in Gaza. I saw a woman "for rent" and decided to spend the night. Those locals thought they could catch me, so they surrounded their own city and fell asleep, expecting to grab me at the gate in the morning. The problem was, in the morning there was no more gate. I had torn it off and walked away with it in the middle of the night.

The next creature to turn up my thermostat was a Philistine, beautiful of course, by the name of Delilah. We were just getting to know each other, and I had basically moved in. Life would have been cozy, except my enemies were still after me.

I found out later that they offered Delilah a lot of money to find out the secret of my strength. I fooled her once, twice, three times until the little game was no fun anymore for either one of us.

She started to beg and plead. And then she said—you guessed it—"You don't really love me." It was my undoing. I didn't want to lose my little plaything, and I was weary of all the whining, so I told my secret.

"No razor has ever been used on my head because I have been a Nazirite set apart to God since birth. If my head were shaved, my strength would leave me, and I would become as weak as any other man." Surely she would realize how much I cared for her and drop the subject.

I fell asleep on her lap, feeling warm and relieved. I woke up to the sound of my name and saw that the Philistine officers surrounded us. I was ready to give them their lesson once and for all, when I realized something had changed. My hair was gone. My strength was gone. The Spirit of God was gone.

They grabbed me and gouged out my eyes. They shackled me and put me to work grinding like a donkey in prison. That was a few months ago. The man who loved the limelight is now weak and blind and forgotten.

I've been here in my darkness waiting for one last chance. I think this is it. The place is packed with Philistines today. They're having a party in my honor. Not for a wedding. Or a gold medal. Or a spectacular victory. They're gloating. They think they've got me because now they're sure I can't get them.

But they don't know God.

My hair has been growing back. Nobody seems to have noticed. I've done their little show and let them laugh at me. I'm beyond humiliation now. One of the servants just propped me up against a support pillar. If I can push hard enough, the whole building will collapse.

Just one more chance, Lord. They gouged out my eyes, and I want revenge. I'll kill myself doing it, but I need your strength one more time. Here goes. One, two, three . . .

TAKE ANOTHER LOOK

Samson was full of contradictions. He was a Nazirite. We see in Numbers 6 that a Nazirite is somebody (usually an adult) who has made a vow of separation to the Lord and must remain holy and consecrated to God for a specific period of time. During that time he must not eat any fruit of the vine or become ceremonially unclean. No razor should touch his head. There is a whole ceremonial ritual to be followed if the person in question accidentally comes in contact with anyone or anything that might make him unclean, including corpses and call girls.

Being a Nazirite is a little strange, but Samson was a strange Nazirite. He was to be consecrated to God from birth, so he didn't have any say in the matter. He was to remain ceremonially clean, but he killed thousands of men, as well as eating honey taken out of the corpse of a lion. He was God's choice for defending Israel, but he broke about every commandment you can think of. He was used by God but had none of his character. He got a special strength from God, but most of the time it looked like he was throwing a big temper tantrum.

Samson was chosen by God, but he made a mess of his life.

> *Many a man thinks he is buying pleasure, when he is really selling himself to it.*
>
> —Benjamin Franklin

A Passion for Passion

Samson's engine ran in overdrive. He was continually revved up. He was a thrill seeker, adventuresome, daring, and impetuous. He was a loud-mouthed womanizer that the guys outwardly hated and inwardly envied. If he lived today, he would drive a fast car or a motorcycle and play extreme sports. He would be the life of the party, until he got mad.

Have you ever met anybody like Samson?

Have you ever been like Samson? What happens to you when you're feeling wired? Do you ever do things when you're overexcited that you later regret? Try to think of a situation when you got too emotional and lost control.

_____

_____

Hold that thought. We'll come back to it.

What are some examples of earthly passions in Colossians 3:5? _____

How does Paul describe a life that resists passion in Titus 2:2–8? _____

_____

What is his advice to the young pastor Timothy in 2 Timothy 2:22? _____

What does it mean to "flee" or to say "no" to worldly passions? _____

_____

How could you have acted differently in the situation you described that you regretted? _____

_____

Driven by a Sex Drive

How do you know that Samson had trouble controlling his passions in the area of sexual morality? _____

_____

The woman he wanted to marry was not an Israelite, so that was one point against him. And he loved her when he saw her. Face it, he did not want this woman just because she could cook. Even after the wedding fiasco, his period of abstinence didn't last long before he decided to go back and get her.

When that didn't work out, he found a prostitute.

At the end of the story, of course, we find him in Delilah's lap. She wasn't an Israelite. She was crafty, greedy, and . . . beautiful. Samson's criteria hadn't changed.

God knows what we're like because he made us. He knows what it feels like to live in a teenager's body because he did. And I'm sure Jesus prayed for his own purity and then put a lot of energy into his schooling, his carpentry, his friendships and family ties. Remember, he wasn't just waiting until he was married; he knew he would never be married.

Urges are urgent, and putting them on hold requires deliberate action.

Read 1 Thessalonians 4:3–5 and 1 Corinthians 6:18.

How does God say we should react to the temptation of sexual immorality?

_____

Why? _____

_____

Samson lusted, and Samson took what he wanted. And his craving for physical satisfaction led to his eventual downfall. This is obviously not how God wants us to live—not only to avoid hurting others but for our own good.

What are some of the ways you can ensure that you avoid this sin?

* _____
* _____
* _____
* _____

Did you mention any of these ideas?

* Decide now that you will not have sex before marriage.
* Avoid pornography at all costs.
* Do not surf the Net late at night or when you're alone in the house.
* Choose your movies, music, and books wisely.
* Choose your friends wisely.
* Do not dress, talk, or move provocatively.
* Fill your thoughts with the Word of God.
* Stay active—homework, youth group, part-time job, sports, hobbies.
* Do not date a non-Christian.

Anger

God endowed Samson with superhuman strength and used that force for his own purposes. God planned to use Samson to deliver Israel from the Philistines. Samson, however, was an impetuous bully. God's motives were just and right. Samson's, on the other hand, were selfish and vindictive.

Every time Samson showed his strength in a spectacular (read "violent") way, he was in a fit of rage. This was a boy with a temper. A bad temper. So bad, in fact, that in Judges 15, even his own people didn't want to have him around. He was too unpredictable.

Take a look at what the Bible says about anger:

Proverbs 22:24 _____

Proverbs 29:11 _____

Ephesians 4:26 _____

Now take a look at yourself. Are you an angry person? Do little things tick you off? Do you say and do rough or violent things when you are irritated?

The next time you feel the heat rising and you're about to blow your cool, what can you do to avoid saying or doing something hurtful?

_____

_____

You're going to say that anger is OK because Jesus got angry. Sure he did. He was angry because God's temple was being defiled; God's name was being insulted. David got angry with Goliath for the same reason. Can you really say that the last time you got angry, it was because you burned with the desire to defend the name of God? Aren't we all a little more like Samson, burning to defend our own causes and maintain our pride?

In every case we see, up until the very end of his life, Samson's anger boiled for revenge. Look what God says about vengeance:

Leviticus 19:18 _____

Deuteronomy 32:35 _____

Romans 12:19 _____

Has somebody hurt or insulted you? Let it go. Don't try to return wrong for wrong. Anger and bitterness will eat away at your bones, and you'll end up paying for it.

Self-control—a Better Way

To the Samson in all of us, the Bible repeatedly says to rein in those passions, master our emotions, and choose with a clear mind to do what is right.

You are reading this in a rational state of mind. You are not in a situation where your feelings could carry you away. But sometime today or tomorrow or the next day, your adrenaline will flow, and you will have to control your emotions so you don't do something you'll regret. Get ready.

Learn 1 Peter 1:13 by heart so you can repeat it the next time you feel yourself shifting into overdrive. *"Prepare your minds for action; be self-controlled; set your hope fully on the grace to be given you when Jesus Christ is revealed"* (1 Pet. 1:13).

CHAPTER SEVEN
LOOKING OUT FOR NUMBER ONE

Delilah's Story
(JUDGES 16:4–31)

I'm on my way to a rather spectacular banquet. The Philistines are celebrating the capture of Samson, and I'll probably receive some kind of honorable mention. The poor guy is blind, so at least I won't have to look him in the eye. It could be a little uncomfortable after all that went on between us.

Maybe I should start at the beginning.

I'm the independent type. I can take care of myself. I've got my own house and my own money, which is rather unusual for a young woman. I like it that way because I can do as I please. I live in the valley of Sorek, which is nestled between the Israelite and Philistine lands and gives me the best of both worlds. I take what suits my fancy. You'll see what I mean.

Being an attractive girl (if I do say so myself) with a few years experience in the ways of the world, I was getting rather bored with the men who came my way. I had it all and could snare just about anybody I wanted. But after a while they were all the same.

Until I heard of Samson. He was a long-haired Israelite who made the headlines on a regular basis. Every once in a while he would go on a rampage and kill men or wild animals with his bare hands. He had been married once, or almost, but he played a riddle game at the reception that ended in a nasty slaughter, an angry groom, and a brokenhearted bride. The bride was later given to the best man, and Samson's relationship was over. And surely in the twenty years he fought for Israel, he knew many other women. Let's face it, this guy had sex appeal. He was wild, handsome, strong, . . . and single. That's a challenge I was ready for.

His wife had been a Philistine. So was the woman he met at the gate, before he walked off with the gate. So I was sure my race and religion wouldn't be an obstacle. It didn't seem to matter to Samson.

Well, I won't bother with all the details of our seduction game, but suffice it to say that I got him. What a hunk! I was so excited at first. I loved running my fingers through that long hair, feeling those muscles ripple in his chest—you get the idea. He was bad tempered and unpredictable, but not with me. He loved me. He said so. And I believe he really did, or he would never have given in to me. I had the poor guy wrapped around my little finger.

That, of course, took some of the fun away. Even this little fling with wonder boy was getting stale, and I needed a new challenge. When my Philistine friends came and asked me to help them capture Samson, I had a feeling this would be my next adventure. My first question was obvious: *What's in it for me?*

The answer was more than enticing: 1,100 shekels of silver, from each of them. That much shiny metal would weigh more than I do and would be worth a considerable fortune. I would be rid of the boyfriend, popular with the Philistine men, and set up for a long time—some kind of retirement planning!

This was the plan: I would find out the secret of Samson's strength. Then I would somehow trick him into losing it. The Philistines would capture him and use him. They didn't want him dead; his muscle was worth too much to them. They just wanted him out of commission, so to speak. We had the mistaken idea that it had something to do with tying him, so that's how we started our "investigation."

I used the direct approach. I asked him straight out: "Tell me the secret of your great strength and how you can be tied up and subdued." I don't know what he thought of me, but I know what he thought of himself. He was invincible. That's more than a notch above good self-esteem.

So he played along. He said to tie him with seven fresh thongs, or bowstrings, made of animal intestines. It was the perfect number and the perfect cord. Or so we thought. The Philistine rulers brought the thongs and then hid behind the furniture. I tied up Sam, cried, "The Philistines are upon you!" and watched as he stood and stretched, snapping the thongs like thread.

I wanted that silver, and I always get what I want. I accused him of lying to me and asked again how he could be subdued. He said to tie him with new ropes. I did. I shouted that the Philistines were coming. He yawned, and the ropes fell off.

I admit I resorted to a bit of whining at that point. And it seemed to work. He came up with a scheme so quirky that I was sure it had to be the truth. He said to weave the seven braids of his hair into the fabric being woven on the loom. So while he slept, I shoved the loom up to the head of the bed and did a few more rows on my blanket with lover boy's hair right in there. It spoiled the pattern, but hey, I could buy another blanket for all that silver. And this one would surely be quite a conversation piece.

I woke him with a shout, and he raised his head—loom, fabric, and all—and pulled out the pin that held it all together.

The Philistines were losing confidence in me. My relationship with Samson was strained. And my future prospects were starting to look dim. I had to pull out all the stops. I had to do something to get what I wanted.

And so I played the emotional female. I whimpered and cried and nagged. I said, "If you really love me, you'll trust me with your secret." I sulked and sighed day after day. And finally, he gave in.

When he told me that he was a Nazirite, that no razor had ever touched his head, that his strength was in his long hair, I knew it had to be true. I called my Philistine friends, and this time I was so sure of myself, they brought their silver with them. I put my little puppy to sleep on my lap again and had one of the officers shave his head.

This time when I woke him up, the Philistines really did come at him. He jumped up as if he was ready to take on the whole army single-handedly, and then I saw a look of panic in his eyes. He had lost his strength. He knew it.

The visitors grabbed him and tied him up. This was one battle they had been dreaming to win for a long time. I turned away when they gouged out his eyes. Then they dragged him off, and the house was quiet. I grabbed the pouches of silver and started counting.

A-h-h, success is so sweet.

As for poor Samson, his romantic days are over. He's in Gaza, grinding in the prison—the damp, dark, lonely prison. The news spread quickly, and the celebrations started immediately. I think even his own people are relieved to know that their unpredictable, uncontrollable defender is in solitary confinement.

In fact, this one arrest has become an issue of national pride. And that's where the banquet comes in. The Philistines have organized a huge party, and Samson will be the guest of honor. From what I've heard, thousands of people will be there when they bring him out and show him off. They'll just use him for cheap entertainment. When they're done laughing at his misery, they'll send him back to prison.

At one time he had a lot going for him. I guess he just didn't play his cards right.

Not like me . . .

TAKE ANOTHER LOOK

Delilah had no idea what awaited her at that banquet. The Bible doesn't actually say that she was present, but it's hard to imagine she would be overlooked on the guest list. That "celebration" ended with the roof caving in and everybody being crushed. Delilah did not get the last word; God did.

Delilah had some admirable qualities. She was not subject to her passions in the way Samson was. She was more rational and well organized. She was able to administer her own budget and her own affairs. She must have been charming because she was trusted by a lot of people (meaning "men"), even when she continually proved herself untrustworthy.

But Delilah's strengths became her weaknesses and her downfall. It can happen so easily.

Rational became selfish and calculating. Businesslike became greedy. Charming became manipulative. And Delilah became a jerk.

Delilah Was Selfish

Clear thinking is commendable when the goal is a righteous one. Driving with your eyes wide open will help you get where you're going. The question is: *Where are you going?* Delilah wanted to maintain control of her own life, and she was willing to plow through despite any moral or spiritual objections to her conduct. Anybody she hurt along the way was just roadkill, so to speak.

God calls that attitude "selfish ambition," and he has some pretty straightforward things to say about it. What do these verses say to Delilah, and to us?

James 3:16 _____

Philippians 2:3 _____

Galatians 5:19–21 _____

I hope you noticed that selfish ambition keeps pretty bad company. Re-read Galatians 5:19–21 and list the other "acts of the sinful nature" that you think Delilah indulged in.

_____

_____

Selfishness is obviously not the foundation of virtue. Looking out for number one can quickly lead to a lot of moral compromises and eventually a very lonely—not to mention godless—end.

Delilah Was Greedy

The problem with being overly concerned about one's own welfare is that selfishness—wanting to satisfy one's own desires—backfires. Selfishness leads to greed, which is the problem of never being satisfied. The more you have, the more you want. Your needs grow, stretch, expand to the point that they can never be met. And, like any addiction, you will sacrifice more and more of your values, relationships, and dignity in the pursuit of unattainable fulfillment.

The New Testament writers seem to be thinking of Delilah when they talk about greed, because they always put that sin in the same pot as one of Delilah's other vices. Can you tell which one?

Check out 1 Corinthians 6:9–10, Ephesians 5:3, and 2 Peter 2:14._____

Greed and adultery have a few things in common. Think about it.

- Both begin with an unreal, exaggerated sense of need.
- Both involve wanting/taking something that is not yours.
- A person always wants more, is never satisfied.
- Greed and adultery ruin relationships by sacrificing other people's happiness in search of your own.
- Getting things and getting pleasure directs your life.
- There is no satisfaction possible.

Delilah had everything, almost. She didn't have the Hebrew he-man. When she got him, she was probably very proud of herself. For a while.

Then she wanted more. She managed to make a lot of money by betraying her lover. And how do you think she felt then? Maybe self-satisfied. But for how long? And what would be next?

Getting off the exhausting treadmill of greed and immorality is called contentment.

The Contentment Solution

What do you think *contentment* means?

_____

_____

The dictionary defines *content* and *contented* as "having the desires limited to whatever one has: not disposed to complain or grumble" and "easy in mind, satisfied especially with one's lot in life." Does that sound like you?

In what circumstances are we told to be content?

Philippians 4:11–12 _____

1 Timothy 6:8 _____

Hebrews 13:5 _____

Contentment means pleasure and satisfaction. No wonder Paul writes to his young protégé Timothy that *"godliness with contentment is great gain"* (1 Tim. 6:6).

If Delilah was a "1" and Paul was a "10," where would you fit on the contentment scale? _____

Do you grumble and complain about your lunches, your pay (or lack of it), your brothers and sisters, your physics teacher, your pimples, your long nose or your short legs? Are you convinced that you need something else to make you happy? Would you be willing to do just about anything to get it?

Let's try a reality check here. Some people in the world would be happy if they got enough bread to make it through the day. Others have food but no homes. Others have homes but no peace. Others have food and shelter but no toilets, no phone, no cars, no electricity. Some people drink the water their animals bathe and defecate in. In some countries you would be working the streets or working in a sweatshop for a few cents a day just to help feed your family. In our own country some children are beaten, abused, abandoned.

Now what was it you were complaining about?

Take the time right now to count your blessings and thank

God for all the amazing people
and comforts that surround you.

_____

_____

_____

_____

_____

I hope you ran out of room.
Write a neat list and stick it up
in your room where you can
look at it often and add to it.

Delilah Was Manipulative

Delilah was *selfish* because
she lived for herself. She was
greedy because she always
wanted more for herself. She was *manipulative* because she used
other people for herself.

> *Contentment is a pearl of great price, and whoever procures it at the expense of ten thousand desires makes a wise and a happy purchase.*
>
> —John Balguy

The Philistine men knew Delilah. They challenged her to
betray Samson by saying, "See if you can lure him into showing
you the secret of his great strength." Can't you just hear Delilah?
"*If?* What do you mean *if?* I got him in the first place, didn't I?
Of course I can lure him, or my name's not Delilah."

Delilah was a flirt, a temptress, a beautiful woman who knew
how to use her charm. There are many ways to manipulate, but
sex appeal is one of the most effective, and the most dangerous.

Listen in on what the wise father says to his son in Proverbs
5: *"For the lips of an adulteress drip honey, and her speech is smoother
than oil; but in the end she is bitter as gall, sharp as a double-edged*

sword. . . . Keep to a path far from her, do not go near the door of her house, lest you give your best strength to others and your years to one who is cruel" (vv. 3–4, 8–9).

Samson would have done well to listen to that advice.

When you notice someone using his or her physical charm to get attention, walk away before you take one step into sinking sand.

And be very careful about the signals *you* are sending: dress, move, and talk in a way that will attract people to *Christ*.

There are other ways to use and hurt people besides sexual manipulation. What are some of things we need to look out for according to these verses?

Job 36:18 _____

Romans 16:17–18

(esp. v. 18b) _____

2 Peter 2:1–3

(esp. v. 3) _____

Do you use sex appeal, flattery, money, or deceit to get what you want from other people? If you are an expert at getting your own way, beware. Manipulation comes from Satan. He smiles every time one person abuses another.

Then again, the Father of Light rejoices every time one human being sacrifices his own interests to meet the needs of another.

Living for Others

The French refer to Delilah's kind of self-centeredness as "thinking you are the belly button of the world." Paul has a practical menu of attitudes and activities to help us forget ourselves,

> *Flatter me, and I may not believe you.*
> *Criticize me, and I may not like you.*
> *Ignore me, and I may not forgive you.*
> *Encourage me, and I will not forget you.*
>
> —William Arthur Ward

and "look to the interests of others." We'll call it the "one another" method.

Choose two of these "one another" principles and think of something you can do to put them into practice:

Serve one another. *Figure out what somebody else's need is, and go out of your way to meet that need* (e.g., I will help John set up his new computer on Thursday night). Your turn:

_____

_____

Forgive one another. *Get over that grudge, and treat the other person as if the offense never happened.*

_____

_____

Encourage one another. *Use God's truth to help a sister grow in her Christian life, remind a discouraged brother of our hope in Christ.*

_____

_____

Bear one another's burdens. *Listen and act to help relieve somebody else's suffering or stress.*

_____

_____

Honor one another. *Treat somebody else like a King's kid.*

_____

_____

Kiss one another. *Acknowledge warmly the family ties we have in Christ. Are there some people at church you haven't smiled at or said hi to for a long time?*

_____

_____

The Bible also says to be devoted to one another, accept one another, exhort one another, tolerate one another, submit to one another, and then some. Anybody that does all of these things does not have a lot of time left over to get hung up on himself.

Jesus sums it up this way: *"A new commandment I give you: Love one another. As I have loved you, so you must love one another"* (John 13:34).

There it is—another "one another." Can you come up with one or two more practical ways to show compassion and kindness this week?

Love one another.

_____

_____

_____

_____

CHAPTER EIGHT
ADDICTED TO EVIL

Jezebel's Story
(1 KINGS 16:29–22:40, 2 KINGS 9:22–37)

They say I'm evil. I say I'm smart. They say there's only one God. I say they don't know the half of it. They say I'm doomed. I say I have a lot of years ahead of me to prove them wrong.

After all, I've proved them wrong before.

Those Israelites have a lot of petty rules and narrow-minded practices. Their whole charade is so disgusting that I decided to move in and break down their intolerance—by wiping out their religion completely. I have come pretty close. And I'll keep trying. The gods are with me, and I will spare no one who tries to oppose my plans.

Like I said, I'm smart. So I started at the top. I married the King of Israel, Ahab. He was a pushover. He hadn't, after all, seen this legendary crossing of the Red Sea with his own eyes, and he was ready to get some support from whatever spirits were available to help him out. That's my department. I introduced him to Baal, the head honcho of a flock of lesser deities, and he was clever enough to see the advantages of a god whose standards were a little looser. We were living in Samaria, and so a temple was built with an altar to Baal in our hometown. It was huge, and it was popular. Ahab also set up an Asherah pole, a kind of monument to another god who is fond of poles.

My next job was to eliminate those tiresome religious fanatics who called themselves prophets. I killed them off like flies and enjoyed every minute of it. In fact, if it weren't for Obadiah's hiding them, and Elijah's slipping between my fingers, I could have eliminated the whole lot of them.

Elijah was sort of the prophet's prophet. When he spoke, they all listened. If they only knew the voices I hear and the dead souls that come back when I call them, I might be able to get a little more respect from them too. My consolation is that the people are starting to see things my way.

Elijah came to my husband one day to say that the land was going to dry up. There would be no dew or rain for three years. Of course his God did set up a little restaurant for the teacher's pet down at the Kerith Ravine, but I only heard about that afterward. If I had known before, I would have cooked his goose long ago. At least we could have avoided that embarrassing showdown on Mount Carmel.

After a three-year holiday Elijah came back to the palace, and Ahab was shocked that he had the gall to show his face. It seems his little visit was to deliver a personal invitation to a contest on Mount Carmel. Elijah wanted a confrontation of the gods, or of their prophets. He invited all my closest buddies—the 450 prophets of Baal and 400 prophets of Asherah who ate in my palace every day.

So the rendezvous was arranged. All the prophets of Baal against all the prophets of Israel's God. That would make it 450 to one. The only downside to this spectacle was that for some reason no girls were allowed. These guys were my little pets, and I couldn't even be there to see their day in glory—their last laugh against the pathetic Elijah.

Maybe I should have been there, because something went terribly wrong. I still don't understand. I know that Baal answers me. I feel his power, his thirst for revenge, his hatred of him they call Yahweh. But that day he didn't perform. Maybe we sent the wrong prophets. Probably Elijah had the whole thing rigged.

First he asked for two bulls to be sacrificed on two altars on the mountain. One would be offered to Baal, and his prophets would ask for Baal to send the fire. The other would be offered to Yahweh, and the Lone Ranger prophet would call to the empty sky and ask for fire. This is where the magic went wrong.

The prophets of Baal cut up their bull and put it on the wood. They chanted and called and danced. Then they screamed and hollered and cut themselves until they were beginning to resemble the poor bull. And they kept yelling. But nothing. The old scoundrel Elijah started to taunt them, as if the almighty Baal had taken a coffee break.

Finally, around the middle of the afternoon, Elijah set up an altar with twelve stones for the twelve tribes of Israel. Unfortunately for him, nobody else from all those tribes seemed particularly favorable to his demonstration. He arranged the wood, cut up the bull, and placed the pieces on the altar. Next he called for water. Did he think if he watered it, the altar would grow? Anyway, he soaked the whole thing, which is an unsavory sight when you consider the bleeding carcass.

He cried out to heaven and bam! Fire came down, burned the offering, burned the wood, burned the stones, and dried up the water in the trench. That is an incantation I must learn. His display was so convincing that he was able to rally those fickle Israelites around him. In a rush of religious frenzy, they cried, "The Lord—he is God! The Lord—he is God!"

Elijah ordered the people to grab the prophets, who were rather weak from loss of blood and unable to resist. They dragged them down to the valley and killed them by the sword—all of them.

When the whole sorry episode was over, rain came. It was about time too. And so it was raining when Ahab came back to the palace to tell me in detail the events of the morning. I was furious of course. If all those men couldn't take care of one measly little rabble-rouser, I would have to do it myself. I should have done it long ago.

I sent a messenger to Elijah to deliver a note of "congratulations": "May the gods deal with me, be it ever so severely, if by this time tomorrow I do not make your life like that of one of them." I must have been the first person with any spine ever to stand up to him, because he disappeared. I vowed to catch him someday, even if the king couldn't.

I was starting to get the impression that there might be a lot of things the king couldn't do. I had married a coward. That was obvious a little while after the Mount Carmel fiasco. There was a simple opportunity to affirm his authority, but he just didn't have the guts to do it. Some commoner by the name of Naboth had a nice little piece of garden property adjoining our palace. Ahab wanted to buy it. Naboth was not selling. So my poor husband, the king, began to pout. It was pitiful.

"Jezebel to the rescue again." I was off and scheming. I sent a copy of my plan to all the officials in Naboth's town, signed my husband's name, and sealed them with my husband's seal. It worked like a charm. Naboth was tried, found guilty, and stoned to death—all in one afternoon.

Ahab just had to claim the vineyard, which he did.

Then guess who showed up out of nowhere? Elijah came marching into the palace with a supposed message from his God: "In the place where dogs licked up Naboth's blood, dogs will lick up your blood—yes, yours!"

But that's not all; Elijah was on a roll. He had a little word for me too: "Dogs will devour Jezebel by the wall of Jezreel." Ha. That's what he thinks.

Then Ahab went out to battle Aram. He was killed in battle. A random arrow struck him, and he sat bleeding all day in his chariot. In the evening he died and was buried. When they washed his chariot, dogs surrounded the little pool and, guess what—licked up his blood.

That was a long time ago, and I'm still here. No dogs, no blood. And happily no Elijah. There's a story going around about him going up to heaven in some sort of flaming chariot. The Israelites have such vivid imaginations.

My son Joram became king of Israel and was carrying on very nicely with the worship of Baal and the practice of witchcraft. I personally think he inherited my gift. But then some young upstart named Jehu showed up one day and said that it was his turn on the throne.

He blamed my son for following in his mother's footsteps. They tell me that Jehu asked Joram, "How can there be peace as long as all the idolatry and witchcraft of your mother Jezebel abound?" And then he shot him through with an arrow.

The news just arrived that Jehu is in Jezreel. He's on his way over to see me. I don't imagine it's a neighborly call. I'll just paint my eyes, arrange my hair, and wait. You'll see. I'll still be here tomorrow, by the power of Baal.

TAKE ANOTHER LOOK

Jezebel was obviously not a nice girl. Some blame her for wearing the pants in the family. Others suggest that her claim to fame is that she's the only woman in the Bible who is cited for wearing eye makeup. But the Avon lady she was not.

Let me hazard a guess that Jezebel's problem went deeper than bossing her husband or coloring her eyelids. In fact, this violent, scheming, godless woman had two major flaws. What are they? (Read 2 Kings 9:22, if you don't remember.)

It's interesting that idolatry and witchcraft go together. Try to give a definition of each and figure out why that is.

Idolatry _____

Witchcraft _____

Why they go together: _____

_____

This association happens in other places too. Check it out in some of these verses:

> For rebellion is like the sin of **divination,** and arrogance like the evil of **idolatry** (1 Sam. 15:23).
> The acts of the sinful nature are obvious: sexual immorality, impurity and debauchery; **idolatry** and **witchcraft;** hatred, discord, jealousy, fits of rage (Gal. 5:19–20).

Jezebel Worshiped False Gods

We'll look at idolatry and witchcraft separately to help us understand what Jezebel's problem was.

First of all, why on earth did a king in Israel actually build a temple to a false god? God says that Ahab "did more evil in the eyes of the Lord than any of those before him." He made Jeroboam's sins look like child's play. Jeroboam started the people on the slippery slope of idol worship, and Ahab more or less made a sport of it. Jeroboam didn't actually deny the existence of God. He just adapted the worship practices so they would be more convenient. He built an alternative kind of church in his own town, so that people wouldn't have to go too far away to worship. Then he made a couple of golden calves, which sounds strangely familiar, doesn't it?

> *Man is certainly stark mad: he cannot make a flea, yet he makes gods by the dozens.*
>
> —Montaigne

From worshiping God the wrong way to worshiping the wrong God, the switch is easy.

And Ahab jumped in with both feet, thanks to the influence of his pagan wife, Jezebel—number one fan of Baal and all his prophets.

What's the big deal? Go back to the basics, the Ten Commandments, and copy the first two (Exod. 20:3–4).

_____

_____

_____

Paul in the New Testament says something very similar. What is it? (1 Cor. 10:14) _____

Is God intolerant? Does he have the right to be? Why? (These verses might help you: Deut. 32:16–18; 1 Chron. 16:26.)

_____

Do you have any idols? Easy question, right? Let's try again. What do you worship? Who or what do you find awesome, exciting, worth imitating, worth making sacrifices for? What do you think about all day?

_____

_____

It could be a hobby, money, a relationship, sports, popularity, the Internet. . . .

God wiped out a lot of people the day Moses came down from the mountain and found them dancing around the golden calf. He is a jealous God. He wants to have all of your attention and admiration.

Jezebel Practiced Witchcraft

Jezebel didn't have a Ouija Board. She didn't read her horoscope or have her palms read. She did play around with the same forces that are behind those things.

Jezebel practiced witchcraft. Nothing is said here about a broom, a cauldron, or magic potions. In fact, God paints a clear picture of what a witch is in Deuteronomy 18:9–12, and we get the feeling we have read about this person in our local newspaper rather than in a fairy tale. In fact, other than the part about sacrificing your children in the fire, you probably have somebody like this sitting near you in geography.

Read Deuteronomy 18:9–12 and list the activities of witchcraft.

- _____

- _____

- _____

- _____

- _____

- _____

"Anyone who does these things is detestable to the Lord!"

When Moses gave the Law of God to the people, he also included the command, *"Do not practice divination or sorcery"* (Lev. 19:26). And just to show how serious he was, he added this stipulation in Leviticus 20:27:

_____

_____

_____

God takes the practice of witchcraft very seriously, which is why Satan loves to make it look like a harmless diversion. Many occult practices involve talk of God, of peace, of doing good. There is a frequent link to ancient or current world religions and holy books. New Age practices of relaxation and meditation are used to encourage people to empty their minds. The door to questionable practices can be opened through games such as Dungeons and Dragons or Magic Cards, or the fascination with Gothic dress and activities.

There are two basic types of witchcraft: divination and magic. Divination is the practice of foretelling the future; and business is booming with psychic phone services, astrologers, and fortune-tellers.

Magic is an attempt to modify reality. A person tries to connect with evil or good powers to move objects, heal diseases, solve mysteries, and cast spells.

Have you ever dabbled in any of these activities? Do you go to occult-themed movies or listen to satanist music? Do you hang out with people that do?

This is not "just for fun." This is witchcraft. Just to make sure you got it the first time, what is God's opinion of all of that "harmless" recreation?

_____

(Any of these words come to mind—*despicable, abhorrent, abominable, revolting* . . . to name a few?)

Consider whom you want to serve. If it is God, he must rule alone. You need to reject radically any game, club, entertainment, or activity that is related to witchcraft. Read the example of the new believers in Acts 19:18–20. What did they do when they came to Christ? _____

Sign your initials here if you are willing to commit yourself to stay away from witchcraft: _____

Jezebel Had No Standard for Behavior

When the people of Israel got tired of waiting for Moses and made a golden calf, they started to party. This was not fun, food, and fellowship. This party was X-rated. They got drunk. They committed acts of violence and sexual immorality. And you know what? The golden calf didn't say a word! It wasn't until Moses came down the mountain with the Ten Commandments from the true God that they felt any shame for their evil acts.

In the New Testament Paul had to deal with the Corinthian society where the worship of pagan gods involved temple prostitutes.

The true God is holy, perfect, transcendent (look it up if you don't know what it means; it's a good word). He created us in his image to be like him, and that sets a high standard of behavior.

An idol is just the reverse. Man is corrupt, finite, and selfish. Man makes a god in his own image. And that invented god can permit and promote just about anything. If we get tired of him, we can just change him for another one anyway.

Add to the very sloppy system of worship and practice the fact that Satan himself is behind every false religion, every occult practice, and every man-made god. You can't exactly expect the devil to deal in holiness.

It should come as no surprise that Jezebel was a violent, thieving, selfish, vindictive woman.

Jezebel Sided with Satan

It is interesting that Jezebel never acknowledged the existence of the devil, and neither do most occult practitioners. Only outright Satanists openly admit to using his power and serving him.

Unfortunately Satan won't go away, even if we try to ignore him. He is alive and well, at least for a little while longer. He knows his end is coming, and no amount of eye makeup will change his fate; but in the meantime he's hopping mad. And he's after you.

Read John 8:44, Ephesians 6:11–12, James 4:7, 1 Peter 5:8–9, Revelation 12:9–10 and answer these questions:

What is Satan doing? _____

_____

_____

What can you do about it? _____

What are some ways you can resist the devil? _____

_____

_____

_____

Pray now and every day, asking God to arm you in your battle against Satan.

POSTSCRIPT

When we left Jezebel, she was in Jezreel, hanging out an upstairs window.

On the ground Jehu called out for help. A couple of bouncers sent her flying to her death, and guess what—the dogs ate her flesh.

God was right. Baal was wrong. It always works out that way in the end.

CHAPTER NINE
TOO BIG TO OBEY

Saul's Story

(1 SAMUEL 9–28)

I didn't realize a little mistake could do so much damage. They say the higher you climb, the harder you fall. And believe me, it hurts. A white-haired prophet just told a great king he was on his way out.

It all started when my dad lost his donkeys. Really. He sent me to find them. Donkeys are slow and stupid. How far could they be? Far enough that about six counties over, I suggested to my servant that we head back before my dad got worried.

My servant said that a man of God lived nearby, somebody who could speak for God and find donkeys. I wasn't very religious, but this sounded convenient.

On the way into the city, we ran into this very prophet, Samuel, who invited us to a sacrifice, told us where to find the donkeys, and said my family would be superblessed—all in one breath.

Nobody could fool me. Things don't work like that in Israel. You have to be born into importance, which generally means priesthood, and I was just a big boy from a little clan in a little tribe.

The next morning, Samuel pulled me aside and poured oil on my head. He said, "Has not the Lord anointed you leader over his inheritance?" To top it all off, he said I would meet a group of prophets on the way home, be filled with the Spirit of the Lord, and start prophesying. Well, I didn't take him seriously. This was a donkey hunt, not a pilgrimage, and I certainly had no intentions of ruling or prophesying.

A funny thing happened when I turned to leave Samuel, though. I began to believe. I felt different. I wanted to see what God could really do. Was I amazed! The best part was when we met that group of prophets. They say it was the Spirit of God. All I know is that I joined right in and started glorifying God with the rest of them. Nobody was more surprised than I was.

Samuel came back a week later as he had promised and called a general business meeting for all of Israel. He explained why the nation was changing administration. God had always been in charge, but now the people wanted a king, and the Lord was willing to work with that. It was time to choose that man. A king, a ruler, anointing, choosing a man . . . I started to put the pieces together, and I got a sinking feeling in the pit of my stomach. So I hid behind the suitcases.

They cast lots to find the will of God, and you guessed it. My tribe was chosen, then my clan, then my family, then me. I was a little easier to track down than a herd of lost donkeys. They pulled me out and pushed me in front of the crowd and started shouting, "Long live the king." That was me. Saul of Benjamin became the first king of Israel. Talk about overnight success. Of course when it first happened, I didn't think I deserved all that honor, but I quickly came to realize that God had chosen the right guy. I was big. I was strong. And I was *good*.

For starters, I rounded up over 300,000 warriors practically overnight and routed the Ammonites. That was just to quiet the doubters in the crowd.

Next we got into a bit of a squabble with the Philistines. Samuel said he'd be there in seven days, but he didn't show. At least, I didn't think he would, so I made the sacrifices myself to get God on our side. Well it seems that was a breech of protocol. Samuel arrived, upset, saying I had disobeyed. God didn't want me to be king anymore, and he would choose somebody else.

When we were back on speaking terms, he said to attack the Amalekites and destroy everything and everybody. So we attacked the Amalekites and destroyed everything and everybody . . . except the king, the good sheep and cattle, the valuable stuff.

Samuel showed up again. "Where's all the racket coming from?" he asked. Of course it was that grade-A beef and lamb mooing and bleating in the field.

We had another argument about obedience. I said I did what I was told, and I just wanted to hang on to a few of the best so I could make sacrifices. But that didn't convince the prophet. He proclaimed my fate, again. "You have rejected the word of the Lord, and the Lord has rejected you as king over Israel!" I cried and begged for forgiveness and mercy. I wished I had one more chance to listen and do what was right. But it was already too late.

I became miserable—so miserable that I longed for those days when God was with me. In fact, I felt like I was being haunted. My staff started to get nervous because I had a nasty tendency to skewer the closest thing alive when I got mad, and I got mad a lot. They brought me a musician to calm my nerves. A harp player. A harmless shepherd boy named David. I liked his music and decided to keep him around.

I should have been suspicious when they said that this kid had the Spirit of God with him. Was it a coincidence that about the time I lost it, he got it?

Not long after that a big brute named Goliath led the Philistine army against Israel. He challenged anyone to fight him who dared, and of course, without the power of God, I didn't dare. And without being three feet taller, neither did any of my men. One day my little harp player showed up, picked up some stones, yelled something about the name of God, and fired. Goliath went down, and David's popularity shot up.

He very quickly moved in with me, made friends with my son Jonathan, and became a commander in the army. Everything was running smoothly until I heard the cheers outside my window. They were singing that David was better than Saul. The little shepherd more popular than the king? I had to do something.

I started with the direct approach. I ordered my staff to kill him. But that didn't work. So the next time he played for me, I threw my spear at him. He dodged it. I sent my men after him. He dodged them. I went after him myself. He dodged me.

I tried everything I could think of, but still he eluded me.

It was so bad that he almost got his hands on me instead. Once after visiting the little boy's room in a cave, I found out that David had been hiding in the back of the same cave. He cut a piece of my robe. He could have killed me. I said I was very sorry.

Another time he sneaked into my camp while I was sleeping and took my sword and my water bottle. I said I was very, *very* sorry. I was mostly sorry that he had outsmarted me. And scared that the next time he wouldn't be such a gentleman.

Things weren't going well on the battlefield either, and I was becoming desperate. So I did something illegal. Something abominable. I consulted a witch. I asked her to get Samuel (who had been dead for years) to come back and talk to me. Now you're going to tell me that spirits don't really come back. The devil just puts on a show sometimes to fool us. I didn't quite understand how it worked when I went to see the witch. But she certainly did. She called up Samuel, expecting a demon in disguise, and she got . . . Samuel!

I asked for his help, but the ghost-prophet immediately brought up the old story about the Amalekites again. The kingdom would be taken from me and handed to David. (Why was I not surprised?)

And then came the clincher. This dead guy looked me square in the eye and said, "Tomorrow you and your sons will be with me."

That was yesterday.

I'm going out to fight the Philistines. I have to. I don't think I can get myself out of this one. But what's the use? I used to be a nobody, loved by God. And then I became a somebody, abandoned by God. Samuel said all God wanted was obedience.

I had my chance. By tonight it will all be over.

TAKE ANOTHER LOOK

Saul could have been a great king. He was God's first choice. All he had to do was obey.

But as his self-confidence grew, his heart shriveled. Before long he figured he could handle things his own way. Where did he go wrong?

Saul Did Not Understand Obedience

Obedience went out of style a few years back. We talk more
about respect now—respecting yourself first and then others,
including endangered species, visible minorities, criminals, victims, the rain forest. You name it; it's somebody's cause.
Listening to and obeying authority has gotten lost in the shuffle.

If you want an interesting exercise, open a Bible concordance
and look up *obey, obeys, obedience*. Mine says that the word shows
up at least 123 times. Apparently the term is still fashionable in
God's books. Saul would have done well to understand why. So
would we.

Look at King Hezekiah for a minute, and see if an example
helps. Read 2 Chronicles 31:20–21 and copy down other
expressions in these verses that explain the term *obedience*. ____

_____

"Everything" is a key word here. Saul went in the general
direction that Samuel pointed him in, but he had a maddening
tendency to adapt his instructions to his own liking. And he
could do some fancy footwork to explain it too.

Can you?

"Well, yeah, I meant to take out the garbage, but you see I
was working on my social studies project, and I knew you didn't
want me to go to bed too late, and so I thought . . ."

"Look, Lord, I'm not going to marry a non-Christian, and
I'm not even going to get serious, but she does like me, and she's
cute, and I need somebody for the prom, and even if we go out
a few times before, that doesn't really mean anything and . . ."

"I know we're supposed to be honest about everything, but
this is different . . ."

There's a great passage in Romans 6 that paints a picture of just how far this obedience thing goes. This is a long one, but it's worth it. Start at verse 11 and read all the way through to verse 19.

What is that *s* word that keeps cropping up? _____

Does a slave pick and choose which instructions she will follow? Does a slave negotiate? Does a slave consider himself wiser than his master? _____

The last phrase of verse 13 is a great definition of obedience. Write it here. _____

What do you think it means? _____

_____

Saul figured he was OK because he was not doing anything blatantly evil. Samuel said that wasn't good enough. Doing what *you* think is best can be dangerous. Follow God's best, without arguing. It's a tall order, and one that only a slave can fill. And that means accepting that somebody else is boss.

Saul Didn't Follow His Master

If you are a slave and God is your master, how do you know what he wants?

For starters, obeying God means following his instructions. They're called his commands, laws, decrees, words, precepts, statutes, and gospel; and the Bible is full of them. Obviously this is not some kind of blind faith. God lays out very clearly what he expects of us. We don't have to read between the lines. We just have to do it.

That sounds fair. It's just God and you and the Book, right? You have no other master, or do you?

> *It is much safer to obey than to rule.*
>
> —Thomas à Kempis

There's a flip side to obedience that might seem a little (or a lot) more difficult. This God whom we must obey requires that we also obey parents, teachers, earthly masters (your boss, your government), and spiritual leaders. He expected Saul to listen to Samuel.

It's a kind of delegated authority. Deuteronomy 32:46 expresses it so well. God said to his people: *"Take to heart all the words I have solemnly declared to you this day, so that you may command your children to obey carefully all the words of this law."*

To whom was God talking? _____

(I hope you said "the adults.")

Who were the adults supposed to instruct? _____

Therefore, to obey the Word of God, the children were responsible to follow the instructions of _____

Paul says, "Children obey your parents in _____" (Col. 3:20).

In an interesting parallel he expresses it this way: "Children obey your parents in _____" (Eph. 6:1).

When your mom asks you to mow the lawn, she is not exactly pronouncing an oracle from heaven; but the authority she has comes from God, and you had better listen.

Saul Became Too Big

Saul started out as a big boy who felt little inside. He believed the prophet, he believed God, and obedience came automatically.

But somehow the power went to his head, and his crown size expanded a few notches. He wasn't so bad after all. God was smart to have chosen him. In fact, maybe he could bend the rules a little and show God a better way of doing things.

What Saul did was offer a sacrifice. Sounds spiritual enough, doesn't it? The problem is, he chose the time, the victim, and the "priest"—himself. The second major blunder came with the attack on the Amalekites. He couldn't bring himself to leave all that gold and those great animals behind. Or the king, for that matter.

Saul's ideas may seem smart. But God had a different plan. Saul was supposed to wait for Samuel to make the sacrifice. He was supposed to kill the king and leave the cows behind. Obedience means rejecting my ideas and following God's. He leads. I follow.

That kind of unquestioning obedience comes from a humble heart—the conviction that God is big and we are small.

How do we know that Saul began his kingly career with a humble heart? (1 Sam. 15:17) _____

John the Baptist is another example of a humble heart. What does Matthew 3:11 say about him? _____

John was the greatest of all the prophets, and he said he wasn't worthy to carry Jesus' footwear. He was small. Jesus was big. In fact, as the crowds that had been following John began to turn toward Jesus, John said with satisfaction, *"He must become greater; I must become less"* (John 3:30).

Could you say that?

Take a look at who you are—a creature who was crafted and brought to life by a powerful Creator. He is the potter. You are the clay. He is big. You are little.

Saul Lost His Faith and His Love

It is humbling to realize that you are the creature of a powerful Creator. You are also a sinner that needs a Savior. Only God can forgive you and give you eternal life when you put your faith in him.

What is the natural outcome of placing your faith in God? (Rom. 1:5; 2 Cor. 9:13) _____

If you believe, you will obey.

What other aspect of your relationship with God will lead to obedience according to Nehemiah 1:5, John 14:23, and 1 John 5:3? _____

If you say you love God, keep his commandments. When the relationship is right, obedience is the natural outcome.

Humility leads to faith, which leads to love, which leads to obedience. Or is that faith first, then love, then humility, then obedience? Or is that obedience leads to faith, love, and humility? Sound like the proverbial chicken and the egg?

The prophet Micah stirs it all together this way: *"He has showed you, O man, what is good. And what does the LORD require of you? To act justly and to love mercy and to walk humbly with your God"* (6:8).

Obedience, love, faith, and humility—it's a package deal.

Saul Didn't Enjoy the Benefits of Obedience

God seems to be driving a hard bargain here. Not always getting my own way. Listening to my parents and teachers. Driving under the speed limit. Following my boss's instructions to the letter. Reading the Bible and doing what it says!

Is it worth it? You bet.

Go back to the example of King Hezekiah. Read 2 Chronicles 31:20–21, but copy only the last four words. _____

_____

_____

In Isaiah 1:18–20, God promises two major rewards of obedience:

Your sins will be _____

You will eat _____

God speaks severely yet tenderly to his people in Exodus 19:4–6, saying, "If you obey me fully . . ."

You will be _____

And you will be _____

Saul was a good guy with a bright future when he was a humble man obeying a great God through the instructions of his prophet.

When he started working for himself, he began a downward spiral. When he went out to his last battle, he knew that it was too late. He had wasted an incredible privilege and ruined his life.

What about you?

Are you convinced that God knows better than you?

Have you put your faith and trust in him to forgive your sins?

Do you love him with all your heart?

How would you rate your obedience on a scale from 1 to 10?
____

How would your parents rate it? ____

Your best friend? ____

Your history teacher? ____

Your youth pastor? ____

The police officer who follows your car on Friday nights? ____

In what area of your life do you have the most difficulty with obedience?

_____

What are you going to do about it? _____

_____

_____

CHAPTER TEN
WASHING AWAY RESPONSIBILITY

Pilate's Story

(MATTHEW 27:11–26, LUKE 23:1–25,
JOHN 18:28–19:16)

I don't know how I got myself into the middle of that one. And weaseling my way out wasn't easy. It's too bad Jesus had to die, though. He seemed innocent to me. But it's not my fault. I did what I could; I didn't really have any choice. At least the emperor's not mad at me. Those religious fanatics aren't mad at me. And the crazy mob isn't mad at me. And believe me, that's not an easy thing for the Roman governor of Judea to pull off.

These Jews are a difficult bunch. They have their sacred writings, what they call the Law and the Prophets. The problem is, their law is not law here. Rome makes the laws. And I have been assigned to this territory by Rome to make sure the people stick to that.

Enforcing Roman law is a big enough challenge. Preventing the Jews from enforcing their own law is another story. You see, in their famous guidebook, there are rules against things like blasphemy and adultery, and the penalty for committing such crimes is death. But blasphemy and adultery are like sports for the Romans. We decide who is put to death around here, and we don't have any time to waste prosecuting the party animals. We go for the mass murderers and political rebels.

This has made some of the really religious types—they call themselves the "Sanhedrin"—very angry. They want to play God and govern everybody's private morality, but we don't let them go around stoning people.

The Jews are also very dedicated to their so-called Sabbath and feast days. In fact, they brought me this man Jesus at Passover, their most important feast of the year. The city of Jerusalem was overflowing with pilgrims who had come to celebrate the holiday.

Their leaders were obviously very determined to do away with Jesus, and they came to get my help. Those two-faced, no-good troublemakers! The same guys that had always complained that Rome was overruling their religious practices were coming to me and asking me to do just that. They alleged that this seemingly harmless man had committed blasphemy. They weren't willing to deal with it on their own, even after I told them I would look the other way. They wanted a Roman death penalty for someone who had not broken any Roman laws. And they wanted it without a fair trial.

When they saw I wasn't interested in getting involved, they started adding new charges. The whole thing sounded fishy to me. They blamed him for advocating a boycott on taxes. Wasn't that the problem we had been having with the Sanhedrin all along? Now they wanted to get rid of Jesus for that very reason? Not likely. They said he claimed to be a king and was therefore a threat to Caesar. That, from a poor tradesman, was hard to swallow, but it was my job to investigate anything that might threaten the emperor. I called Jesus inside to question him thoroughly.

What an unusual man.

I asked him directly if he was the king of the Jews. He answered that he was a king but that his kingdom was not of this world. Caesar could sleep in peace as far as Jesus was concerned. He may have been strange, but he was no threat to Rome. I still couldn't quite figure out why the priests hated him so much.

I took Jesus back out to his accusers and said the obvious: "I find no fault in him at all." That should have been the end of the whole story.

But as I spoke those words, I looked out across the group that had turned into a crowd—people who had obviously been rounded up by the Jewish leaders. They started circulating rumors and accusing Jesus of more and more ridiculous crimes. They were getting louder and angrier. This was a problem that was not going to go away.

And through all of this high-energy hostility, Jesus just stood there. He was so obviously innocent, and yet he never spoke a word in his defense. I wished I would wake up and find that the whole scene was just a bad dream.

It may sound like an easy mess to get out of: send Jesus home and go back to bed. That would have been plan A. But it wasn't so simple.

I hate these Jews. I have from the very beginning. And when the governing jobs got passed around, I just had to be the one to end up with the province of Judea of all places. My job is to enforce Roman rule on people that are extremely set in their odd ways and try to keep the peace between their priests and our king. Both, of course, are stubborn, proud, and power hungry.

I have done everything to prove to the emperor that I can handle the rabble-rousers, and I have tried over and over again to enforce Roman law. But it's just not working. Somehow I always end up in hot water. It seems that Caesar is getting rather weary of hearing stories about uprisings and revolts. I am supposed to be keeping the peace.

So when I looked out at the mob, I knew this wasn't just another day in court. My career was on the line here. If I didn't give them what they wanted, they could cause me more than just a headache. They could cause a scene that would cost me my job.

Then I heard one little word that came to me like a life preserver to a drowning man—"Galilee." This guy was from Galilee? What a relief! Galilee was not in my province. If Jesus was really from Galilee, I could ship this whole mess over to Herod, and then whatever happened would be his fault, not mine. Herod just happened to be in Jerusalem. Plan B was a stroke of genius. Or it seemed so at the time.

As the procession headed over to Herod's, the crowd got bigger and louder. Was I ever relieved to be getting rid of this case! Conveniently for me, Herod had a particular interest in seeing Jesus. A few years earlier he had a run-in with Jesus' cousin John the Baptist, who had accused Herod of immorality and made one very mad governor. Well, more specifically, one very mad governor's wife. After John was arrested, Herod's wife put her own daughter up to asking for John's head on a silver platter, and she got it. Herod did not seem too scrupulous about eliminating a Jewish troublemaker now and again. This would be perfect.

I found out later that after questioning Jesus and getting no answer, Herod decided to play games. He dressed him as a king and made fun of him. When this cheap little entertainment started to lose its flavor, Herod shrugged his shoulders and sent Jesus back to me. He was in the same fix I was.

That meant Jesus' case ended up back in my lap. And the crowd was getting bigger and angrier all the time. Plan B flopped, so I had to go for plan C. Every year at Passover, I release a Jewish prisoner—a token of peace and goodwill, if you will. If I gave these people a choice between the scummiest prisoner, somebody they hated, and this quiet teacher called Jesus, surely they would see clearly enough just to let Jesus go.

Being the diplomat I am, and willing to make compromises, I also offered to have Jesus flogged—that meant beating with a Roman scourge. He would be stripped, tied to a post, and whipped with leather thongs with bits of glass and bone stuck in the end until his flesh was torn open. Maybe then the crowds would be satisfied. I was still looking for a way to avoid the death penalty.

Just as I was feeling the pressure rise to a breaking point, my wife appeared. She said, "Have nothing to do with this just man, for I have suffered many things today in a dream because of him." As if I needed that!

All I had left was the prisoner-release deal. I was sure they wouldn't choose Barabbas. So I gave Jesus one last chance. "Which of the two do you want me to release to you?" I called out to the crowd.

"Barabbas!" they answered.

"What shall I do with Jesus?"

"Crucify him!"

I was dumbfounded. I'd been had. I had no Plan D. I had no choice. So I washed my hands in front of the raging mob and said, "Do it. It's not my fault."

TAKE ANOTHER LOOK

We live in a world of Pilates. We blame our parents, society, and our myriad of disorders and diseases for our behavior, rather than owning up to our own actions. Nothing seems to be anybody's fault anymore.

Pilate was bulldozed into a dilemma that he did not want. Circumstances pushed him way out of his comfort zone. But he still had a choice. We always do. He made the wrong one.

Pilate Did Not Choose What Was Right

Pilate's job was to rule, to see that justice was done. Sounds simple enough, but Pilate failed. The difference between right and wrong somehow got lost in his search for easy. Faced with an obviously innocent man, he eventually gave his consent to crucify him.

Look up these verses and find the words that describe doing the right thing: 2 Samuel 8:15, Psalm 99:4, 11:7, Proverbs 1:3, 21:3, and Jeremiah 4:2.

_____

_____

What three things does Jehosophat warn against when speaking to the judges he appointed? (2 Chron. 19:7) _____

_____

A striking command is given by God to Moses, recorded in Exodus 23:2. What would the onlookers at Jesus' trial have done differently if they had paid attention to God's instructions? What about Pilate? _____

_____

_____

Good and evil do exist. In God's scheme of things, there are absolutes. The world may be confused, but God still says, "Do not kill, do not steal, and do not commit adultery." Every man must choose to do right, no matter what others around him are doing.

Pilate Feared Men Rather than God

It's interesting that Jehosophat begins his instructions to judges with the admonition: "Now let the fear of the Lord be upon you." Then they would be able to judge carefully.

Some would say that the word *fear* means "respect." But then why would God, in other circumstances, say, "Do not fear"? Surely he does not mean, "Do not respect." What is the place of fear in Scripture? Should we be afraid of God? See if you can come up with some words to describe the attitude or feeling that is referred to in these verses, when ordinary people encounter an extraordinary God:

Luke 8:36–37 _____

Luke 5:8–10 _____

Mark 5:33–34 _____

Mark 4:41 _____

Isaiah 6:1–5 _____

What is it about God that's so scary? _____

_____

(Maybe Luke 12:5 would help you here.)

God is love. He says we can call him "Dad." He is our father, our brother, and in many ways, our mother. He is a God of compassion and grace. But before you get the idea you can walk all over him, consider this. He holds the planets in his hands. He is holy, incapable of tolerating one little blot of sin and selfishness. He controls nature, and he controls your destiny. He made the rules, and he expects you to play the game his way. When there was a storm outside their boat, the disciples were afraid. When the storm stopped, and they realized that God was *inside* their boat, they were terrified! No wonder.

If you are starting to get comfortable with God, maybe you need to read about his encounter with Job, in Job 38–41, or some of the ultimate praise songs in Revelation, such as 15:3–4. Truly our God is an awesome God.

In a little twist that only God could pull off, fearing him is connected to many other Christian virtues and benefits. See if you can tell what they are.

Psalm 147:11 _____

Deuteronomy 6:13 _____

Psalm 2:11 _____

Psalm 111:10,
Proverbs 9:10 _____

Proverbs 10:27,
Proverbs 19:23 _____

Proverbs 16:6,
Ecclesiastes 12:13 _____

Fearing God means wisdom and long life and blessing, but it also means serving him and obeying him. And it means that when the pressure mounts, I choose my popularity with him over my popularity with people. Pilate should have ignored the crowd, refused to be swayed by the anger of the Sanhedrin, and disregarded the risks to his career. He should have declared Jesus innocent and let him go. He had the power to do so. He might have felt cornered, but he still had a choice.

Can you think of any situations where the pressure is on you to compromise your values? Describe one or more here.

_____

_____

What is Paul's point in these verses: Galatians 1:10a, Ephesians 5:8–10, and 1 Thessalonians 2:4?

> *In matters of conscience, the law of majority has no place.*
>
> —Mohandas Karamchand Gandhi

_____

_____

Even if it is hard today to see the benefits of risking all to please God rather than men, Paul puts it into perspective for us in 2 Corinthians 5:9–10. What awaits each one of us (v. 10)? __

_____

Choose one of the situations you mentioned, and write a game plan to help you do what is right. *I will* _____

_____

Pilate Didn't Take Responsibility for His Own Actions

Pilate has the dubious distinction of making irresponsibility famous. When we do not want to take the blame, we say, "I wash my hands of this." Did you ever wonder where we got that expression? Now you know.

Refusing responsibility or, even worse, blaming somebody else, is as old as sin itself. When God called out to Adam in the garden, Adam said Eve had given him the forbidden fruit. Eve blamed the serpent. And God cursed all of them. He knew exactly the role that each one had played.

And he knows exactly what choices you and I make.

We are in a society where parents make excuses for the children: "Oh, he must be tired." Teachers make excuses for their students: "They're really good kids on the inside." And the law makes excuses for criminals: "He wasn't really aware of what he was doing."

Probably the most famous example of ridiculous responsibility-shrugging is the "Twinkie" case. A San Francisco City supervisor, accused of murdering the mayor and a fellow supervisor, explained to a sympathetic judge that he had a junk-food addiction. The more he ate, the less control he had over his actions. This was particularly true when he ate too many Hostess Twinkies. Which, of course, was the case before he killed his victims. This line of defense actually saved him from a first-degree murder conviction and lessened the charges to manslaughter. Poor helpless murderer had been in the throes of a Twinkie rush, and he just didn't know what he was doing. It wasn't his fault. Sounds pretty far-fetched, doesn't it?

What are the first words that come to your mind (or mouth) when your mother asks you to clean up the mess in the living room? When your professor asks why your assignment isn't completed? When the police officer asks why you were driving so fast? When somebody sees you blow your cool and asks, "What's wrong with you?"

If you're anything like me, you can weave a story that would sound good in a campaign

> *Each snowflake in an avalanche pleads not guilty.*
>
> —Stanislaw J. Lee

speech. You can turn things around so that you're the victim rather than the villain. If you're really good at it, you might even end up as the hero.

Somehow, we've got it figured out that without a crime there is no guilt. Without guilt there are no consequences. Think again. The Bible tells a different story.

1. Sin is real.

Sorry Pilate, but you condemned an innocent man. That was unjust. It was a sin. But you're not alone. Nobody has a perfect record. In fact, the Bible says just the opposite.

Refresh your memory by noting what these verses say about Pilate, you, and me:

Ephesians 2:1 _____

Romans 3:23 _____

1 John 1:8 _____

Isaiah 59:2 _____

2. Because we have sinned, we are guilty.

This is not just a bad feeling but true guilt. We deserve to be punished. Check these out for proof of that:

Romans 6:23 _____

2 Corinthians 5:10 _____

Deuteronomy 24:16 _____

Going to therapy to get rid of guilt feelings is a popular but ineffective solution to true guilt. If you have sinned, you are guilty. God has the only solution.

3. The only way to get rid of guilt and truly avoid the consequences of sin is to own up and ask forgiveness.

By trying to keep himself out of trouble with Caesar and the people, Pilate got himself into trouble with God. He washed his hands as he was soiling his soul.

True "clean" comes with a clear conscience, a right relationship with God and others. God cannot forgive sins that you don't admit you've done. If you're willing to face up to them, his promises are sure.

Psalm 130:3–4 _____

1 John 1:9 _____

If you have done something wrong and would like to pretend it never happened, don't. Try this instead. Name your sin. Confess it to God and ask him for forgiveness. Pray for those you may have hurt. Make restitution where necessary. Then forget it. God has. Go in peace.

Read Psalm 51, which is David's prayer of confession after he finally admitted that he had committed adultery and murder.

Write your own prayer of confession here:

_____

_____

_____

_____

CHAPTER ELEVEN

FORFEITING FAITH FOR FOOD

Esau's Story

(GENESIS 25:19–34, 26:34–27:40)

I am a down-to-earth kind of guy. I like fresh air, good food, and fair treatment, which is something that seems to be sadly wanting in this conniving family of mine.

In fact, from what I hear, Jacob, my scheming little brother has been out to get me since the very beginning—*before* the beginning in fact. My mother says my twin brother and I started to fight before we were born, as if we knew or cared who would be born first. Well, I was, but Jacob came out with a good grip on my heel. This was not touch football. This was serious competition.

Being the firstborn son in Israel means a lot. It was a distinction that my brother had his greedy heart set on since that first tight wrestling match. The birthright means inheriting a double portion of the family estate. It also gives a position of authority to the eldest male over the whole clan, including his brothers and their children. So far so good. The part that I don't get is the family priesthood and the patriarchal blessing.

Some families have household gods, little statues to remind them of a supernatural power that guides and protects them. The greatest honor to bestow on a child is to pass these gods on to him. My family worships an invisible god, and that faith was passed on from my Grandpa Abraham to my dad, Isaac, and from Isaac to me. Because the family's faith was passed to me, I would have to teach my own offspring and the nieces and nephews about him, so that each generation would know and believe.

All that religion stuff is a bit too much for me. I'd rather be in the woods with a bow and arrow than sitting around an altar or a candle pretending to talk to somebody I can't even see.

Religion, on the other hand, is very important to my family. Grandpa Abraham actually saw and heard the angel of the Eternal One. The way my dad tells it, Abraham was chosen by God to be the father of a great nation. That was a covenant. And that was improbable. Grandma was way past her prime, and he still wasn't the father of even one child. But their God did come through, and Grandma and Grandpa had my dad, Isaac. Which meant that my dad carried on the line of covenant. Which means that he will pass on the covenant promise to his eldest son. Which should have meant that this great nation would come from my children. My offspring would inhabit the promised land. I would experience and pass on the presence and blessing of God. There's even some talk about a special heir, a sort of superdescendant, chosen by God, still to come. As far as I'm concerned, the double inheritance is the most interesting part.

This is where Jacob comes into the story again.

Two brothers couldn't be more different. We are twins, but our birthday is the only thing we have in common. I am an outdoorsman. I am hairy and tanned and tough (and my father's favorite, for that matter). Jacob is fair skinned and gentle and would rather cook the meat than kill it. He helps my mom out so much that she likes him better than me.

One day, when I went out to hunt, I had to go a little farther, run and climb and shoot a little more than usual. I lost a few arrows, missed a few prime roasts and drumsticks, and became exhausted in the process. At the end of the day, I dragged myself back to our tent empty-handed. I was tired. I was thirsty. I was famished.

And I was in luck. Having an extra cook in the family comes in handy sometimes. I could smell that lentil stew from way down the road, and it was all I needed to urge me on. The closer I got, the more I drooled. I was a man with a one-track mind.

"Quick, let me have some of that stew!" I cried on arrival. "I'm famished." Jacob had already guessed that by the wild look in my eyes.

His own look was anything but wild. He was cool and calculating. And blunt: "First, sell me your birthright."

Why not? "Look," I said, "I am about to die. What good is the birthright to me?"

Jacob wanted me to swear an oath so I wouldn't change my mind. You've never seen a contract signed, sealed, and delivered so fast. I had no intention of changing my mind. Who needs a birthright anyway?

A piece of bread and bowl of soup never tasted so good. I devoured it. And I went along my merry way, minding my own business as usual.

I eventually got a little lonely out there in the woods all day and thought it was about time I settled down. Since there were no pretty girls around among the cousins, I paid a visit to the Hittites, and found two—Judith and Basemath. For some reason my parents never approved of my wives. It was something about keeping the promises in the family—that religion and covenant business.

The birthright exchange was insignificant for me, but I did not like the idea that the little rat Jacob would get all the goodies. Lucky for me that my dad still preferred venison to beef and kept a soft spot in his heart for his favorite hunter.

As Dad got older, he lost his sight but not his appetite. One day he called me in and asked as a final favor that I go and shoot some wild meat and prepare him his favorite dish. He knew that I was still the eldest son and had some claim to his blessing. What I wanted most was just the assurance that Jacob wouldn't be able to boss me around. I am my own boss, always have been.

I went out that day with a mission. My eyes were sharp, and my steps were light as I headed into the woods with my quiver full of arrows. I was sure I wouldn't need them all. Luck would be on my side.

Unfortunately, it took me a little longer than usual, or maybe it just seemed that way because I was so anxious to get back to my father. And what a shock was waiting for me when I finally did.

I killed an animal, brought it home, cleaned, and cooked it with my adrenaline running high. I was so pleased and relieved to enter my father's tent, expecting one of the happiest moments of my life. It was one of the worst.

I announced my arrival by saying, "My father, sit up and eat some of my game, so that you may give me your blessing." I should have known something was wrong when my dad asked, "Who are you?"

That was when I learned the bitter truth. Jacob had killed a goat and prepared it just the way dad liked it. He came in before me, pretended to be me, and took the blessing. He had been gone only a few minutes.

Now I'm not a man to shed tears, but I shouted and ranted and cried. He couldn't have hurt me more. I begged and pleaded with my father to bless me too, but he had already made Jacob the head of the family. His very words were that Jacob would be lord over me and all the relatives. Imagine!

I was sobbing. "Bless me too, my father!" I insisted. And he tried, dear old man. He tried. But there wasn't much left to give. He had given everything to Jacob—that cheater, that thief, that treacherous scoundrel. He stole my birthright. He stole my blessing.

Now just wait until I get my hands on him! When my father is dead and buried, I'll kill the little runt. I swear it.

We'll just see what good all this talk about God and blessing and covenant can do for him then. I don't need religion. I'll get by. You'll see.

TAKE ANOTHER LOOK

When I read this story in Genesis 25, I wonder, *Why did God choose this family to pass on the covenant? Couldn't he have done any better?*

At first glance Jacob seems worse than Esau. He was a mommy's boy, a schemer, a manipulator, and a liar. He took advantage of his brother's weakness to take his birthright, and he stole the blessing by a theatrical bit of deception toward his dying father.

Not only did this greedy, selfish man behave terribly, but his mother was with him all the way. In fact, she suggested the lie, cooked the goats, and disguised the villain.

This was a dysfunctional family.

And these were the descendants of Abraham, the heirs of the promise, the forefathers of Christ.

With so much wrong, this one thing was right: God chose to be with them and bless them. What made Esau any worse than the others? His behavior? Hardly. But the Bible says he was godless. He chose to reject the blessing.

How can we avoid Esau's mistakes?

Esau Did Not Appreciate His Spiritual Heritage

The Bible says, *"Esau despised his birthright."* He had no idea of the importance of his family's faith, no respect for his parents' values, no concept of the privilege that was to be his.

Some of this nonchalance and ingratitude could be attributed to the fact that Esau's family was rich. The Bible says that Grandpa Abraham was a very wealthy man, and Father Isaac was his heir. Esau was the son of a rich man. He probably had little sense of the real value of work, of material possessions. He was favored by his dad. He was used to being catered to. Esau went hunting because he enjoyed it, not because it was a necessity. The family had flocks and herds in abundance to supply their meat.

It should come as no surprise that being spoiled did not make him grateful. Nor did it make him obedient or respectful. Nor did it encourage him to think about the deeper issues of life.

Considering that Isaac's family was wealthy, we can understand why Esau wasn't too worried about his pension plan. Whether he got a single portion or double portion of inheritance wasn't a major issue.

The real privilege of birthright wasn't the dollars and cents but the blessing and presence. And Esau didn't care. He didn't listen to his father's spiritual teaching. He did not believe. Here was the guy who would have been in line to inherit all the promises of a chosen nation, a promised land, a coming Messiah—and he didn't appreciate any of it.

> *Prosperity is the worst breeder of insolence I know.*
>
> —Mark Twain

Isaac and Rebecca, on the other hand, despite their glaring weaknesses, were right about one thing: the God of Abraham is alive. He keeps his promises. And there is life beyond lentil stew.

The apostle Paul's junior partner, Timothy, was the opposite of Esau. He appreciated the privilege of a godly upbringing.

What does Paul say to encourage him in 2 Timothy 3:14–15?

_____

Who taught Timothy about God? (1:5) _____

How are you doing with your spiritual heritage? Are your parents Christians? Do you listen to them, respect their principles? Have you adopted their faith and made it your own? Will they be passing along the baton of belief to you so that you can pass it to the next generation?

If your parents are not believers, they are still the best parents for you. If you enthusiastically accept and copy all the good things in their teachings and lifestyle, chances are they will listen when you talk to them about Jesus. If you are God's child, he can start a new line of blessing with you that will carry on to your descendants if your children and grandchildren are faithful.

Esau regretted his choices, but it was too late. If you were to invite him to your youth group, what kinds of recommendations

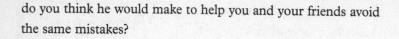

do you think he would make to help you and your friends avoid the same mistakes?

_____

_____

_____

I can imagine him mentioning a few of these:

- Appreciate Christian parents, grandparents, aunts and uncles.

- Respect and obey your parents, even if they aren't believers.

- Imitate the example of godly people.

- Listen to your elders. Their experience can teach you a lot about what's really important.

- Persevere in your faith as you get older.

- Remember that there is more to life than what you can see and taste.

Esau Satisfied His Earthly Appetites

You will be happy to know that God is not against food, water, and rest. In fact, the only saints that don't eat, drink, and sleep are the dead ones. The rest of us need our ration.

When Elijah fell into a great spiritual depression after his victory on Mount Carmel, God did not tell him to pray and read the Pentateuch. He fed him and put him to sleep. Then he fed him again and put him back to sleep. Jesus caused a certain amount of scandal by enjoying himself. And he was such a sound sleeper that he could snore in the bottom of a little boat during a big storm.

Why then does the Bible contain so many warnings about indulging these very natural and legitimate appetites?

The wise man of the Book of Proverbs urges us to work hard like the ant and to avoid laziness. *"A little sleep, a little slumber, a little folding of the hands to rest— and poverty will come on you like a bandit"* (Prov. 6:10–11).

But activity, or lack of it, does not seem to be Esau's main weakness. The devil surely knew that the way to this man's heart

> *You've got to do your own growing, no matter how tall your grandfather was.*
>
> —Irish Proverb

was through his stomach. The following verses do not say, "don't eat," but they all talk about certain dangers connected with eating (other than calories and cholesterol). What are they?

Luke 12:22 _____

Luke 21:34 _____

John 6:27 _____

Notice that it is Jesus himself, the one who has gone to prepare a wedding feast for us, who warns about food becoming an obsession. Esau's problem was not that he was hungry. His problem was what he was willing to give up to satisfy that hunger.

Paul has an interesting angle on this whole idea of restraining the appetites. Copy here what he wrote in 1 Corinthians 9:27: _____

We can be pretty sure that Paul didn't literally whip himself. His enemies took care of that on a fairly regular basis. So let's think about what he means in both parts of this statement.

What does he mean by beating his body? _____

_____

What is the difference between the body being a slave or being the master?

_____

_____

What about you? Are you controlled by your basic needs for food, drink, and sleep, or are you able to sacrifice those things for a higher cause? (This does not mean staying up all night to finish a term paper!) Have you ever prayed all night? Have you ever gone without food or drink so somebody else could have it? Have you ever fasted?

Find the names that belong in this "Fasting Hall of Fame," and see if this is company that you'd like to keep.

Exodus 34:28 _____

1 Samuel 7:5–6 _____

1 Kings 19:8 _____

Ezra 10:6 _____

Luke 4:1–2 _____

Acts 9:8–9 _____

Acts 13:1–3 _____

Acts 14:23 _____

Fasting can be beneficial in a lot of ways. Here are some of them.

- Fasting adds punch to your prayers.
- Fasting is a good way for you to check how addicted you are to your comfort.
- Fasting will give you compassion for the poor and hungry.

- Fasting frees up a lot of time for communion with God.
- Fasting is good practice to help you say no to your urges in other areas.

Jesus said that his disciples would fast when he was gone. Consider practicing this spiritual discipline if you are not already.

Esau Did Not Have an Appetite for God

It's interesting that God endowed each of us with a regular and urgent hunger mechanism, and then he compares spiritual reality to food and drink. Jesus himself says that he is the Bread of life and the source of Living Water. He says, *"My food . . . is to do the will of him who sent me and to finish his work"* (John 4:34).

The Bible also says that our desire for God should be as real as that growl in the midsection. What are the words used in these verses to describe a desire to know God?

Psalm 42:1–2 _____

Psalm 63:1 _____

Psalm 119:131 _____

Matthew 5:6 _____

1 Peter 2:2 _____

Do any of these verses describe how you feel about God? All the time, sometimes, a few minutes per week, only on youth retreats?

If you're like me, this kind of longing, craving, yearning for God doesn't always dominate my thoughts. What can you do to nurture spiritual hunger? Here are some things that help me. You might want to add some of your own suggestions to the list.

- Consider God's power and majesty in his creation.
- Read rich devotional books—Eugene Peterson, Spurgeon, Tozer. Read and meditate on the words of old hymns.
- Set aside several hours or a whole day, once a month, for prayer, fasting, journaling, reading.
- Spend some time with an older person who is in love with God.
- Read biographies of godly people.
- Find regular short periods in the day for praying or memorizing verses—jogging to school, doing dishes, waiting in line in the cafeteria, after the kids you babysit have gone to bed . . .
- Choose your music, reading material, TV shows, computer games wisely. Do not dull your spiritual senses; do not make constant noise in your head.
- Feed yourself on the Bible, Christian entertainment, Christian fellowship.
- Learn the words to Christian songs that challenge you to get to know God better.

- _____

- _____

Choose one or two of these suggestions, and write here what you plan to do about it this week.

_____

_____

CHAPTER TWELVE

MESSING UP THE MISSION

Jonah's Story
(JONAH)

I have a heart for missions as much as the next guy. I go to missions conferences (when there's a meal), I invite visiting missionaries to my house, and I have even sat through a few missionary slide shows. I signed one of those cards at a youth rally that says "Anything, anytime, anywhere." That got me into a little short-term mission stint when God sent me to tell King Jeroboam II to restore the boundaries of Israel. The king complied, and the trip was a success. I figured I had done my part.

When I heard my name coming out of nowhere, it startled me at first. Then I realized it was God and relaxed a little. What more could he expect of me?

"Jonah," he said again. "Go to the great city of Nineveh and preach against it because its wickedness has come up before me."

Nineveh. My head started spinning. My stomach was churning. My muscles were tensing.

Nineveh and wickedness—that much at least made sense. In fact, I thought the Lord was being a little too generous here. The Ninevites were our enemies—a constant threat, an ever-present evil. They were treacherous and despicable. The good news was that God had finally noticed.

The bad news was those other two unthinkable words—"go" and "preach." He wanted *me* to go and preach to *them?*

That's what he said. He wasn't giving me a choice.

I ran away.

I went to Joppa and caught the next boat for Tarshish. He said east, and I went west. I figured God needed some time to rethink this little missionary project of his. And if we couldn't come to an agreement, my answer was clear. I would do anything *but* this. I would go anywhere *but* there. I left on an extended vacation—no forwarding address for visions, dreams, voices, or angelic visits.

Just as I was beginning to enjoy my cruise, God turned on the loudspeaker. I had gone down below deck for a little power nap, and the lullaby of the waves and rocking of the boat put me to sleep like a baby. I missed the beginning of the storm.

The wind was so strong and the waves so high that the sailors thought the boat was doomed. They screamed. They cried. They prayed. They called every god in the book, but nobody answered.

Desperate, they started throwing the cargo overboard to lighten the ship.

That's when the captain realized there might be another god that could be contacted, and I might know how.

The captain roused me from my deep sleep and said we were dying and could I please call upon my God and try to get some help.

First of all, dying wasn't mentioned on the travel itinerary.

Second, God and I were not exactly on speaking terms.

And as the boat began to take on water, I got another sinking feeling. What if the Lord God, Creator of the wind and the waves, was trying to get *my* attention?

Then those sailors, who really were believing types, came up with a plan: "Let us cast lots to find out who is responsible for this calamity."

It didn't take too many tries for everybody else to figure out what I already knew. I had been singled out, and the questions started flying.

"Who is responsible for making all this trouble for us?"

"What do you do?"

"Where do you come from?"

One question at a time. I am a Hebrew, and I worship the God who holds this sea like a little drop in his hand. But right now I'm not really worshiping. I'm not even listening to him. Let's just say he said "zig," and I did a "zag."

The other sailors were smarter than I was. At least they took God seriously. "What have you done?" they cried in panic and astonishment above the roar of the storm.

It was no time to explain that I might have made an error in judgment. I knew these guys didn't deserve to die, but I did.

"Throw me over," I said.

Instead they rowed. That was generous. It just didn't work.

They begged God's mercy and threw me in, half expecting to be struck by lightning. They weren't.

The wind stopped. The waves fell flat. The sun came out. What was left of their boat sailed calmly on. They had a worship service. I thought it would be my funeral service. I couldn't see the shoreline, let alone swim there. It was a good time to pray!

Suddenly, and not a minute too soon, a mouth opened, and

I was, well, swallowed. You ain't smelled nothin' until you've spent three days in a fish's digestive system. Maybe it was my impulsive reaction the first time that gave God the idea, but this time he really had me cornered. I prayed for three days, with my nose plugged.

The fish threw me up on the beach. Was I glad nobody was there to welcome me! I have never wanted a bar of soap and a hot bath more than I did at that moment.

No sooner did I get cleaned up than I heard that now familiar voice: "Go to the great city of Nineveh and proclaim to it the message I give you."

What could I do?

"OK, if you insist," I muttered.

"Pardon?"

"I said, 'I'll go.'"

And I went. The assignment was simple: walk around the streets of Nineveh shouting, "Forty more days and Nineveh will be destroyed." I walked for three days. I shouted until I was hoarse. These guys were my enemies to begin with, so I wasn't exactly expecting a warm welcome. And with the message I had been sent to deliver, my ratings didn't go up any.

Everybody in the city heard the doomsday news—a punishment on Nineveh that I had been hoping for since I was a kid. I should have been happy. But I wasn't.

In fact, those three days were longer than the three days in the fish. The whole time I was telling those wretches that the end was near, I had the feeling God might rewrite the plot.

It turned out even worse than I thought. The more I proclaimed their fate, the more the Ninevites repented. Even the king put on sackcloth and dust. Then he decreed, "Let everyone call urgently on God. Let them give up their evil ways and their violence. Who knows? God may yet relent and with compassion turn from his fierce anger so that we will not perish."

And God did it. As far as I'm concerned, those Ninevites were too far gone, and they deserved the disaster that was coming to them. But for some reason God showed mercy. Deep down I knew he would. I guess that's why I didn't want to come here in the first place.

I wanted to conquer them. He used me to save them. What a disappointment!

There was nothing left for me to do. My life was a failure. My hopes were shattered. I wanted to die, and I told God so. "I knew that you are a gracious and compassionate God, slow to anger and abounding in love, a God who relents from sending calamity. Now, O Lord, take away my life, for it is better for me to die than to live."

I had to stop my complaining because the Lord had a question: "Have you any right to be angry?" he asked.

Yes, of course I did.

I went out of town. I was sick of the sight of those Ninevites on their knees! And I sat down in the hot sun to pout. What would God do to that crowd anyway? As I watched in misery, a neat little green plant sprung up behind me, and the leaves covered my head and gave me shade. I deserved a little relief after all I'd been through. Finally God was beginning to see my side of things. Life might be worth living after all.

I was pretty exhausted, so I slept like a log in my new shelter. The nightmare started when I woke up. A wretched little worm came and ate my vine. The hot wind blew, the sun beat down, and I felt dizzy. Just as I was raising my fist to God to ask, "Why?" he showed up with another of his trick questions: "Do you have a right to be angry about the vine?"

I answered yes. I think I got that one wrong, just like the first one. But I didn't care. I was hot and miserable. I just wanted to die, again.

He asked one more question—not a true or false this time. He compared my vine with the people of Nineveh. He said the old greenery just grew and withered in a day, and I had grown fond of it. Shouldn't he be concerned about 120,000 confused and foolish people and their cows?

Frankly, I can understand the part about the cows, but what is the point of putting up with dumb (not to mention hypocritical, devious, evil . . .) people?

I still think God got it all wrong. But maybe some good can come out of this mess. I noticed Joppa wasn't a bad place. Good weather. Thriving port. No temple, yet. Maybe I could do a little missionary service over there and spend my day off fishing. Because believe me, there are some whoppers out there!

TAKE ANOTHER LOOK

OK, I admit it: Jonah never signed a commitment card or watched a missionary slide show. And nobody really knows where he went after his sad Ninevah episode. But poetic license aside, this is a tale you know. How many times have you heard this story? And why does the hero usually turn out to be the fish?

Jonah was a preacher, a missionary, a believer called by God to proclaim his message.

And he blew it. Catastrophically so.

Obviously, running away was his first mistake. Even when he did listen to God's instructions and follow them, his heart was definitely not in the job. He reminds me of the little kid whose mother asks him to sit down. He wants to remain standing, but he knows the consequences of disobedience, so he complies. As he seats himself, he looks his mother defiantly in the eyes and proclaims, "I may be sitting on the outside, but I'm still standing on the inside."

Jonah was in Ninevah on the outside, but he was definitely in Joppa, or maybe at home in his hammock, or anywhere else but Ninevah, on the inside. To the very end of the book, he never really got it. He was selfish and grumpy. Jonah was honored by a call from the Master, and he pouted. What was wrong with this guy?

> *Evangelism is one beggar telling another beggar where to find food.*
>
> —Source unknown

Jonah Did Not Understand God's Compassion

Jonah knew that God is a compassionate God. He said so. When the Ninevites repented of their evil ways, God forgave them and gave up on his threat to destroy them. Jonah prayed, saying, "I knew that you are a gracious and compassionate God, slow to anger and abounding in love, a God who relents from sending calamity" (4:2). What a privilege, what a joy to serve such a merciful deity! Right?

Jonah continued, "Now, O LORD, take away my life, for it is better for me to die than to live" (4:3). Jonah's theology was right, but there was definitely something wrong with his heart.

The Bible is full of references to God's love, grace, mercy, and compassion. What do these verses say?

Psalm 116:5 _____

Psalm 145:8–9 _____

Matthew 9:36 _____

Feels good, doesn't it?

You can be sure Jonah felt good about God's compassion when it was directed to him. He knew that his own salvation depended on God's mercy.

Compassion is not warm feelings. Compassion does not equal congratulations. Compassion can only be directed to somebody who is lost, weak, even dead.

What will God do for you, for me, because of his compassion?

Psalm 51:1 _____

Micah 7:18–19 _____

Ephesians 2:1, 4–5 _____

The Gospels use the word *compassion* eight times when speaking of Jesus. When he felt compassion, he healed, he touched, he reached out his hand, and he wept.

Jonah forgot that the sin of the Ninevites was no worse than his own. It's a good thing for Jonah, and for us, that God forgives sinners.

Jonah Did Not Share God's Compassion

For God, the connection is obvious. Being the jerks that we all are sometimes, we don't always understand. If you have experienced the love and mercy of God, how can you harbor resentment for another struggler—even if his particular weaknesses happen to grate on your nerves or inconvenience you in your personal comfort zone?

What does God's compassion lead to in these verses?

Zechariah 7:9 _____

Colossians 3:12–14 _____

What of that other girl who's charming all the guys in the youth group? What about a mom or dad who is constantly making you feel like a burden? Then there's the teacher who seems to mark you harder than everybody else. And the guy who stole your CD player from your locker. And the girl who talks about you behind your back . . .

Proverbs 25:21 _____

Matthew 5:44 _____

Luke 6:35 _____

Well, God will understand that I'm not perfect. Sure he loves me (and no wonder!), but what he/she/they did to me is inexcusable. I just can't . . .

What kind of measurement does God use when he requires us to forgive?

Matthew 6:14–15 _____

_____

Ephesians 4:32 _____

_____

Jonah Didn't Understand the Mission

What does 2 Peter 3:9 say about God's love for those who don't know him? _____

_____

_____

And if everybody is going to repent, everybody has to hear, right? Romans 10:14 says, *"How, then, can they call on the one they have not believed in? And how can they believe in the one of whom they have not heard? And how can they hear without someone preaching to them?"* Sounds logical.

If you've been around the church and the Bible for a while, you probably know what we call the Great Commission by heart. Try to write it here. (Peek if you must—Matt. 28:19–20. See Mark 16:15 for an alternate version.) _____

_____

_____

The "all creation" or "all nations" phrase is pretty important. It should have been to Jonah. It should be to us, too.

Jewish Jonah thought he was pretty special. He was a part of God's chosen people. The covenant was with Israel. The commandments were written for the Israelites. The temple and sacrifices belonged to them. The Ninevites were outsiders, pagans, heathen.

King David understood something that Jonah didn't. What was it? (Ps. 96:2–3; 9:11, 67:2) _____

_____

Worshiping God means telling others—around the world—about his great deeds and character.

Jonah Did Not Want to Do His Part

As you read your Bible and try by the Holy Spirit to put it into practice, you also will realize that God has a plan for you that may not be written in black-and-white in its pages. The Word of God is effective in improving your character. As you get to know God better, you also may become convinced of some specific ways he wants you to serve him.

Right after the wonderful declaration of salvation by grace, Paul says this, and it's worth repeating:

Ephesians 2:10 _____

Jonah was assigned a special mission. He almost blew it, but for some reason God insisted on using him.

Jesus says that the job has not yet been completed. The calling and sending didn't stop in Bible times. He says to pray that workers will be sent out to evangelize the world (Matt. 9:38). He wants us to be those workers.

Do you know anything about world missions? Do you know any missionaries? Have you ever thought of going for a short-term mission experience? Do you believe that God wants to use your gifts in full-time Christian service—at home, or in another country or another culture?

What about now? What about here?

If believers could declare the name of God among all nations in the days of foot messengers, donkeys, and fishing boats, people living in the twenty-first century should be able to find the ways and means to communicate something this important.

Can you think of ways a teenager can talk about God to his family members, classmates, total strangers, people in other countries?

_____

_____

_____

Here are some suggestions that might help you get started:

- Talk to your pastor about mission opportunities in your church.

- Go out for a hamburger with a missionary on furlough and ask him/her to tell you about his/her experiences.
- Visit some Web sites of short-term missions organizations.
- Get some information about a missionary family and commit to praying for them on a regular basis. You could write and tell them you're praying and ask them to send you their news.
- Send money or a care package to a missionary family. Be creative. Maybe you could get your family or youth group involved and send a bigger gift.
- Find out about the immigrants in your neighborhood or the international students at the local university. Could you befriend somebody from another country and share your faith with him or her?

What can you do to begin this week? _____

_____

_____

Pray every day that God will send laborers into his harvest. Be ready if he answers, "I want *you*."

CONCLUSION
THE WAY OF WISDOM

People haven't changed much over hundreds—make that thousands—of years, have they? The jerks of today are strangely like the characters we have been looking at in the Bible. And as Solomon describes the flaws of fools in the Book of Proverbs, we see little snapshots of some of the same people.

Was he thinking of Haman when he wrote, "The way of a fool seems right to him" (12:15), or Samson as the "fool [who] is hotheaded and reckless" (14:16)? When Esau rejected the privileges of birthright, Isaac knew only too well that "to have a fool for a son brings grief" (17:21). Jezebel is a prime example of a foolish woman who tears her house down (14:1). When I read, "A fool finds no pleasure in understanding but delights in airing his own opinions" (18:2), I think of Jonah trying to get God to understand his point of view. And that pompous Babylonian king surely proves that, "as a dog returns to its vomit, so a fool repeats his folly" (26:11).

As different as these characters are, they do have one striking thing in common. King David wrote that the foundation of foolishness is refusing to believe in God. Solomon says that even worse than simply not believing in God is believing in yourself. That's a description that fits some of the jerks all of the time and all of the jerks some of the time.

A few of the characters we looked at were children of God. I am a child of God. I hope you are too. I have made the choice to believe, to worship, to follow. And in the big picture, that's how it works out. But I still see Delilah in the mirror sometimes, and Esau, and Jonah . . .

And I realize that it's in those little everyday temptations and choices that I still mess up. I feed my pride. I give in to my feelings. I do things my way. And that's just like saying at that moment in time, "There is no God." Or worse still, "I'm the god around here."

Godlessness is selfishness. Selfishness is godlessness. And at that point I'm no good to myself or to anybody else.

The way of wisdom points us in another direction if we're ready to listen. "Rein in your passions." "Do what is just and right no matter what the cost." "Serve others generously, honestly, and sacrificially." "Obey always." It's a tall order, but the hand that guides us is a steady one. And a forgiving one.

That's why I like the story of Nebuchadnezzar. He was so thick that he kept repeating the same mistake over and over, but after seven years as a king turned cow, he admitted that God was, well . . . God. And he was restored.

That means there's hope for you and me.

As we continue to make choices every day, we will still make some bad ones. But it's not all over. God specializes in redemption, and he will keep working on us, working with us, and working through us.

Solomon has some pretty practical advice about making the right choices, and I think Proverbs 28:26 says it in a nutshell. I'm sure he wouldn't mind if I paraphrased it like this: *"If you do things your own way, you're a jerk, but if you follow God, you'll be OK."*